SIX NATIONS, TWO STORIES

Kate Rowan is a freelance sports journalist. Her passion for sports writing was sparked by her involvement in *Trinity News* while studying at Trinity College Dublin. She has travelled widely, covering the 2011 Rugby World Cup in New Zealand, Ireland's 2012 June tour to New Zealand, and the 2013 British and Irish Lions Tour of Australia. Kate has written features for the *Irish Independent* online and has worked extensively for governing bodies including World Rugby (formerly IRB) and the IRFU. She has covered women's rugby from club to inter-provincial to international level. Dublin born and bred, Kate also spends time with her family in Carrick-on-Shannon

Peter O'Reilly is the rugby correspondent of the *Sunday Times Ireland* and has been reporting on rugby since the game turned professional in 1995. Educated at Belvedere College, he came to journalism via teaching and also spent two seasons on the playing staff at Warwickshire County Cricket Club in the 1980s. In 2004 he wrote *A Full Bag of Chips: Ireland and The Triple Crown*, published by The O'Brien Press, and he has ghostwritten acclaimed autobiographies by Anthony Foley and Johnny Sexton. Peter lives in Dublin with his wife, Cliodhna, and their three children.

SIX NATIONS, TWO STORIES

KATE ROWAN   PETER O'REILLY

THE O'BRIEN PRESS
DUBLIN

First published 2015 by
The O'Brien Press Ltd,
12 Terenure Road East, Rathgar,
Dublin 6, D06 HD27, Ireland.
Tel: +353 1 4923333; Fax: +353 1 4922777
E-mail: books@obrien.ie
Website: www.obrien.ie

ISBN: 978-1-84717-791-9

1 3 5 7 8 6 4 2
15 17 18 16

Cover images and all images in photo sections by Inpho (inpho.ie),
except where indicated.

Printed and bound by Scandbook AB, Sweden
The paper in this book is produced using pulp from managed forests

CONTENTS

BACKGROUND

Kate Rowan

A footnote to the story of Ireland's victory over New Zealand's Black Ferns in the Women's Rugby World Cup in August 2014 is that on the eve of the historic fixture, the Irish belted out 'Let It Go', from the hit animation *Frozen*, which the squad had watched as part of their movie night. This glimpse of life in the World Cup camp struck a chord with the Irish public: the Disney song had become an anthem of overcoming adversity for women and girls all over the world.

The tournament, in which Ireland reached the semi-finals for the first time, was followed by a raft of high-profile retirements, as players such as captain Fiona Coghlan, Lynne Cantwell, Siobhan Fleming, Grace Davitt and Laura Guest left the fold. Head coach Philip 'Goose' Doyle and his management team would be also moving on. In the lead-up to the 2015 Six

Nations Championship (currently sponsored by the Royal Bank of Scotland and officially known as the RBS 6 Nations), new coaching staff, structures and players were introduced. As it happens, a lyric from 'Let It Go' describes this period of transition: 'I'm never going back, the past is in the past!'

Back in 2008, when one of the stars of the 2014 World Cup run, Niamh Briggs, made her Test debut for Ireland against Italy at the St Mary's ground, Templeville Road, the women were lucky to attract more than a couple of a hundred spectators. As Briggs explains, those who did turn up were directly connected to the team: 'It was always just your family and one or two friends ... they were the people that you made come to your matches.' In preparation for the 2010 World Cup in England, Doyle – who first became interested in women's rugby because his wife played – was reintroduced, having been head coach from 2003 to 2006. Over the next four years he guided Irish women's rugby to exciting new highs. Although he coached part-time while also running a business as an electrical contractor, he helped add a new feeling of professionalism to an amateur set-up. According to Briggs, 'Goose, probably reluctantly on his part, was Mr Irish Women's Rugby. His passion and will to win was amazing but not only that, his will to get the best out of players. He was incredibly intelligent in how he went about his business – I loved the fact he was so driven. I loved his honesty.'

Coaching is also a team pursuit, and Doyle created a successful partnership with Greg McWilliams, who worked as attack, backs and skills coach from 2010 while teaching at St Michael's College, Ballsbridge. Briggs credits McWilliams with helping to drive Ireland's women's success: 'Greg, for me, opened us up to a whole new world of rugby. He has great enthusiasm and ability to get his point across. The game plan he gave us was unbelievable. The two of them together worked incredibly well. It is very important to note that both of them did it voluntarily. I owe my success in rugby at the moment to the two of them, in large. It is hard to put into words, you know – I looked up to them so much.

'You have got to remember Goose is married to a lovely girl, Nicola, in Wexford, with three amazing kids, all teenagers, and he was having to leave them every weekend and most evenings. Greg was newly married to his wife and to come every weekend to coach 30 women … I'm sure she was delighted with that!'

During the 2013 Six Nations campaign in which Ireland won their first Championship, with a grand slam, they beat England for the first time in their history. Out-half Nora Stapleton recalls the coverage granted to this match by one national newspaper: 'After the England game I was like, "Surely there will be something on it?" I opened it, scanned the newspaper and couldn't find anything, and the next thing, under a sub-heading … it was "news in brief" and … talked about Johnny Sexton and underneath that … "The ladies beat England." I was like, "Are you serious?" I counted up the words and it was 56 words … A few other newspapers were way better but I was disgusted.' With that grand slam win came a sudden surge of media interest in the women. As Stapleton says: 'You are on the front of the papers. It comes from winning matches. You always know you have to win matches to get attention and for the public to be aware of it.'

With women's rugby's increased profile due to the grand slam and World Cup successes, the team captain and loose-head prop Coghlan became the public face of the sport. However, her value to her team was much more than that, as her front-row colleague Ailis Egan describes: 'She is the best leader, best captain I have ever had and it would be interesting to see if anyone comes close to her. She is very natural. She is not the best player. She is not the best prop in the world by a long shot, but she is by far the best leader in women's rugby. Gill [Bourke] and me would often make fun of her, saying: "Ah here, clearly we are doing all the work because you can't scrummage for shit," but we did take that back after the World Cup. She proved her worth there. For me as a player, she is hugely inspirational and motivational. She would really keep you going. She expects high standards. She'd expect you never to miss a training session. It doesn't matter about your job or what is going on in your outside life. This comes first. That is something I have taken on since she left. That is for me. That is my mantra.'

What would Irish women's rugby be like without the likes of Doyle and Coghlan, who for so long set the standards that led to layer upon layer of improvement?

Heading into the 2015 campaign it was announced that the women's fifteens side would be part of the IRFU's High Performance Unit for the first time, joining the women's sevens programme. Australian Anthony Eddy, who had held a similar role at the Australian Rugby Union, became Director of Women's and Sevens Rugby. Former Ireland international scrum-half Tom Tierney was appointed as the first full-time, fully professional head coach to women's fifteens. Ireland had been punching above its weight in this respect as England, France and Wales all had professional coaches at the 2014 World Cup. Players who were part of the full-time sevens programme, training with the aim of qualification for the 2016 Olympics in Rio, were now eligible to trial and play for the fifteens side, opening up a new pool of talent.

How does one tell the story of Irish women's rugby in 2015?

First, it is important to realise that when looking at the women's and men's teams side by side, you are not comparing like with like. As blindside flanker Paula Fitzpatrick puts it, 'Men's rugby is professional. It is a different game really; the women's game brings something different. I think the men's game is getting so structured now, there is so much analysis in it, and it is quite defensive at times … defences tend to dominate games … women's rugby … can sometimes be more exciting to watch.'

Having covered the men's game, I did not start to write about the women until after the 2013 Grand Slam, so perhaps I could be considered a journalistic bandwagon jumper. This is something I felt a certain amount of guilt about, but my thinking had always been that I wanted to be the best sports journalist I could be, and this meant that I would cover what was seen as the pinnacle of rugby – the professional men's game. It was flawed logic to some extent. I don't believe that it should just be women covering women's sport. Writing about sport, women and gender can become a minefield, as people have such strong opinions around these issues.

I knew that I wanted to tell the 2015 Six Nations story in as authentic a fashion as possible, showing what makes the women's game unique, and to give an insight into what drives these women to sacrifice so much to play rugby for their country. Three types of narrative have often been used in the Irish media to talk about women's rugby, which I personally don't think do the players any justice. The first runs along the lines of 'Ohmigod, rugby is such a butch sport but these girls are actually really feminine off the field and love to wear make-up and pretty dresses!' Then there is the 'our girls' coverage that became popular post-grand slam: rather than crit-icising any aspect of a performance, for example when Ireland lost 7–40 against England in the World Cup semi-final, much of the reaction is along the lines of 'Ah, the poor girls!'. Many of the players do not appre-ciate this, as Stapleton explains: 'The commentary in our matches … is all positive. Are they afraid to criticise us when we play bad or do they not watch the games? It could be one or the other. We know when we play shit and nobody wants to be scathed, but sometimes when we play shit, maybe it is blamed on external factors as opposed to bad passes.' Finally, I have found journalists or commentators who cover women's sports preaching and taking the moral high ground over doing so. This is rather off-putting. There is no point in trying to force people's interest.

Looking back at the people who had taken women's rugby to the point it was at between the 2014 World Cup and the 2015 Six Nations – Doyle, McWilliams and Coghlan, as well as the likes of Briggs and Stapleton – they all had amazing human stories behind them. I wanted to tap into stories like these, but about the Class of 2015, so that even if you have yet to understand fully the intricacies of the women's game, you will be able to connect with the emotional journey. With Irish women's rugby at a crossroads in terms of more professional structures being implemented, the 2015 campaign took women's sport in Ireland into uncharted territory.

This story, like any good sporting tale, has highs and lows, tears and cheers, and tells of how a group of diverse individuals can come together to defy the odds.

2

STEPPING STONES

Peter O'Reilly

IRELAND 22, NEW ZEALAND 24

AVIVA STADIUM, 24 NOVEMBER 2013

This is a story with a happy ending, but for any story to be truly satisfying, our heroes need to have endured some hardship or survived a painful experience along the way. For the current Ireland rugby team, that experience occurred on Sunday, 24 November 2013, when players and fans came agonisingly, heartbreakingly close to uncharted and highly desirable territory: beating New Zealand, world champions and the most successful international side in the history of the sport. Any success that the team has achieved since – and there has been quite a bit – has been driven to some extent by the communal pain suffered on that ridiculously dramatic afternoon in the Aviva Stadium.

The beauty of sport is that the joy and the pain are shared experiences, which bond the team even closer to its supporters. Anyone who was present will have images that linger in the memory. On social media, the most popular picture was a still of the large video screen at the north end of the stadium, taken before we were even halfway through the first half, and reporting a barely believable state of affairs: Ireland 19, New Zealand 0. Never before had an entire rugby nation made a collective attempt to accelerate time.

As a journalist working for a Sunday newspaper, I was already in the largely unfamiliar situation of being able to enjoy the game without scribbling notes and tapping away on a laptop. My week's work – previewing this, Ireland's final game of the autumn series – was already done. No deadlines, no frantic communications from the *Sunday Times* sports desk, just a game to watch. And what a game! What a buzz at the Aviva.

Nothing had prepared us for the shock of being so far ahead of the number one team in the world. Yes, there had been a big sense of expectation when Joe Schmidt had taken over as national coach at the end of the 2012/13 season – hardly surprising, given that he had enjoyed so much success with Leinster, winning four trophies in three seasons. Any time a new coach arrives, he tends to bring an energy that lifts performances. But after a fairly routine swatting of the Samoans on Schmidt's first outing in charge, Ireland had seemed strangely subdued against Australia, eight days before the New Zealand Test. Despite fielding a team that included nine Lions, they went down 15–32 to a Wallaby team that had been experiencing more than a few difficulties, on and off the pitch. Most dispiritingly of all, the tourists scored four tries to zero. Only 45,000 people turned up – 6,000 off capacity – and the Aviva lacked atmosphere.

There seemed little chance that the Kiwis could be caught off guard eight days later. They were battle-hardened, having won Tests in Tokyo, Paris and London in the preceding weeks. As ever, winning was a habit for them. In fact, they had lost only one of their previous 34 Tests. Yes, they would miss Dan Carter, who had injured himself against England, but Schmidt's preparation had been disrupted by injuries too. Up until Friday of that week, there was a very real chance that Johnny Sexton and Brian O'Driscoll would miss the game. Two rookies, Paddy Jackson and Robbie Henshaw, had been told to prepare themselves for battle.

What we didn't know was that Schmidt had targeted the New Zealand game ever since his players had assembled in Carton House at the start of the month. This is not to say that he had taken the Samoans or the Australians lightly; it was more that he had made enormous demands in terms of the amount of technical and strategic information that players were expected to take on board, even implementing different systems of defence for the second and third games in the series, in a successful attempt to outmanoeuvre New Zealand's coaching staff and video analysts. To some, it seemed as if the performance against Australia had suffered from information overload, as if data had dulled the passion. This certainly wasn't a problem against the All Blacks.

For that delirious opening quarter, Ireland had been Leinster at their best, only wearing a different colour – ruthless, relentless and totally irrepressible with ball in hand, blasting black jerseys out of rucks to produce quicksilver ball, which in turn was transformed into tries for Conor Murray and Rory Best. They were also devilishly aggressive in defence, hounding the All Blacks with the sort of intent that led directly to Rob Kearney's memorable 70-metre breakaway try in the 18th minute.

Later we would look back on the finer details of this score – how Dave Kearney's ferocious tackle on Israel Dagg had created the opportunity and how Dave had been first to congratulate his brother; how a determined chase by Kieran Read, New Zealand's number eight, had prevented the elder Kearney from scoring near the posts, which in turn made Sexton's conversion more difficult; how critical this would prove to be. At the time, however, what struck you most in the press box was simply how noisy it was inside the Aviva, especially for a Sunday afternoon at 2.30. Looking back, it seems like this was a moment of awakening.

Up until that point, our lovely new stadium had been a relatively unhappy new home. Since the Aviva opened for business in November 2010, Ireland had played 17 Tests there and won fewer than half – seven wins in total, one draw, against France, and nine defeats. Without making excuses for those results, players privately expressed the view that the stadium had lost the terror that it used to hold for visiting teams when it was plain old, draughty old Lansdowne Road. With so many public amenities in the new stadium, it seemed that punters were spending more of their time at food and drink outlets than they were in their seats, where they could voice their support. Alan Quinlan had expressed this very idea in his *Irish Times* column early in 2013, following the decidedly tame atmosphere during Ireland's defeat by England in the Six Nations. Quinlan had been working for RTÉ Radio throughout the half-time break that day and went for a toilet break as soon as the second half started. As he entered the concourse inside the West Stand, he was 'blown away' by what he saw.

'There were hundreds of people just milling around, standing there having a drink and watching the game on the screens,' Quinlan wrote. 'They weren't queuing for food, they were just standing there looking up at the TV. I couldn't believe it. Why would you bother making the effort to go to the stadium if all you were going to do was stand there and watch it on TV?

'I actually got pretty angry about it. You go to a sporting occasion because of what's happening on the pitch. In a game like this one, where the tide was against Ireland but they were coming back into it how can you just be casually sipping at a drink or picking away at a bag of chips?'

No one was hanging around the concourse as the second half of the New Zealand game began. By that stage Ireland led 22–7, New Zealand having reduced the lead with a Julian Savea try; Schmidt would apportion no real blame to the team's defence on this occasion, seeing the score as the result of some clever anticipation by the wing, who also benefited from a kind bounce. He did think that certain defenders might have worked harder to prevent Ben Franks's try in the 65th minute, but then the entire end-game made painful viewing for a Kiwi who understood that the result of this game had added resonance for both sets of supporters. New Zealanders wanted to put the finishing touches on a calendar year where their team had gone unbeaten. Irish supporters just wanted to put an end to their dismal record of failure against the All Blacks.

Many of us had been in the position of watching Ireland trying desperately to hold onto a lead against this opposition. Back in November 2001, Lansdowne Road was all a-flutter when Denis Hickie scored early in the second half to put Ireland ahead 23–7, only for Jonah Lomu to wreak havoc in the final quarter, and for the tourists to finish 40–29 winners. Then, many supporters seemed content merely to have given New Zealand a fright. Now, it wasn't acceptable to roll over in the final quarter. Ireland were fit enough, and defence was supposedly one of their strengths. It was reasonable to have expectations.

We recall 2013 as a case of Ireland wilting under New Zealand pressure, but it can also be viewed as a case of Ireland protecting a lead when they should have been extending it. This wasn't an isolated case of Ireland drying up on the scoreboard. Against Wales in that year's Six Nations, they had gone 30–3 up early in the second half, only to end up fighting for survival. The previous week, Australia led by just three points at the break, only to pull away after it. And in general, Ireland seemed to have an issue with scoring points in the second half of games.

Here, they didn't score a single point after Sexton's penalty in the 33rd minute. Granted, opportunities were few but they needed to be taken – most notably when the Irish maul squeezed a kickable penalty for Sexton with seven minutes remaining and his team leading 22–17. For some older spectators, this recalled Barry McGann's famous kick to beat New Zealand in 1973, when the game was tied 10–10 – the closest Ireland have come to getting this monkey off their backs. McGann's kick was from a similar angle but there simply couldn't have been the same expectation on his shoulders. Sexton is a professional, kicking in more consistent conditions – more consistent balls, same kicking tee, less wind. With the amount of practice he does and the amount of coaching he receives, kicks from the 15-metre line, even to the right of the posts, count as 'bread-and-butter'. But the tension in the stadium was increased by the knowledge that this angle is not one he likes, and that converting it would leave Ireland two scores ahead. To intensify the pressure further still, he took even longer than normal over the kick, before pushing it just to the right.

Sexton was replaced almost immediately, which practically confirmed the suspicion that he'd been playing through a hamstring niggle. Those who saw him in the dressing room after the game described him as 'inconsolable'. The first time I broached the topic of the missed kick with him was nearly two months later, and he still seemed haunted by the memory. He admitted that he'd had the opportunity to come off nearly 10 minutes before the kick but was reluctant to do so, as Ireland were already short a couple of leaders – Rory Best departed during the first half, having played for several minutes with a broken arm, while Brian O'Driscoll was forced off with concussion, very much against his will.

'Yeah, the call came for me to come off when we conceded the try,' Sexton said. 'But I wanted to stay on. I was still warm and the adrenaline was flowing. I thought I could still make the right decisions for the team.

'In many ways I'm proud that I opted to stay on but I have regrets too. After the game I was thinking "Damn it, I should have just come off." I don't know whether the injuries had an effect. Did I commit fully to the kick? Did I get fully through the ball? It's a regret. I'd been looking forward to that game for a long time and I'd been kicking very well. You look back and wish you got it and wish Ireland had gone on and won and made history. No one has thought about it more than me.

'Obviously, I knew the score. I knew this was to go two scores ahead. But I was just in my routine. I still look at the kick and wonder why it didn't go over. Look, I was probably a bit broken, maybe there was a little bit of a breeze, maybe it was me not getting through the ball. But they're all excuses and I should have got the kick. I missed a kick. I've beaten myself up over it. Now I just have to move on. If I can play a part in delivering a Grand Slam or a Six Nations title, I think you can look back and say that you learned from it.'

There were still five minutes on the clock – minutes in which Ireland would make critical errors, but minutes that would ultimately teach the players important lessons. Cruelly, a couple of younger players, introduced off the bench, were among those caught out. Players like Jack McGrath, the man who conceded the penalty with 29 seconds remaining on the game-clock to give the All Blacks one last glimpse of victory, or Ian Madigan, the last man in the defensive line when Dane Coles put Ryan Crotty over just under two minutes later. In other words, the Irish bench had been responsible for a couple of big errors, whereas the New Zealand replacements delivered when it mattered most.

With the penalty decision, the natural Irish reaction was to question the wisdom of referee Nigel Owens. Owens is one of the top referees in the sport but he has a habit of finding himself centre stage in games that end dramatically. The previous year in Christchurch, he was the man in the middle when Dan Carter had broken Irish hearts with a late drop-goal, seconds after a contentious penalty decision against Ireland's scrum. This time, Irish players wondered how Owens had ignored New Zealand players infringing at the ruck only a matter of seconds before he pounced on McGrath. Schmidt was slow to criticise the ref, however. His players had to be wise to certain match situations and how they would be refer-eed. When a team showed signs of trying to play the clock down with a series of one-pass phases, you had to make sure your technique was whiter than white at the ruck. In technical terms, you had to 'support your own body weight' rather than flop on top of a tackled team-mate. McGrath didn't do that. Owens blew, then uttered the words that have stayed with the player ever since. 'Number 17. Straight off your feet.'

This was McGrath's third Test appearance, but Schmidt wasn't of a mind to make allowances. International rugby is an unforgiving environment. When he reviewed the match with the squad, the 24-year-old prop came in for some stinging criticism. McGrath took it on the chin.

'With Joe being such a stickler for tiny margins and stuff you do in every aspect of your game it's obviously going to get picked up,' McGrath said subsequently. 'Like, it had to be picked up – it had to be. It was a motivating factor for the rest of the squad after that – the last 90 seconds or so. I beat myself up. Like there was no excuse for it. It was a mistake and it just happened so quickly and that was it. It was pretty crap at the time and for a long time after it but again, that's part of sport and you have to pick yourself up. It's only going to affect you if you really dwell on it. I was pissed off for a few weeks but you just have to bite your lip and get on with it.'

If supporters were numbed after Crotty touched down in the left corner, in almost the identical spot where Rob Kearney had scored an hour previously, we can only imagine how the players felt. Green shirts were littered everywhere. As if to tease everyone a little more, Owens checked with his TMO for a forward pass in the build-up to the try, but this brought no joy. The scores were level at 22–22. All that remained was Aaron Cruden's conversion, to complete a perfect 2013. He was wide with his first conversion attempt but Owens gave him a second shot, as Luke Fitzgerald had charged a millisecond early. Cruden nailed it. Of course.

'I think Nigel was compelled to give him another opportunity,' Schmidt said when he met with a group of Sunday journos the following week. 'At that stage, though, for me … it was all about winning this game. A draw had been done before. We had worked so hard to get that 19 point lead. We'd worked so hard to be 22–10 ahead with 15 to go. I did think we were going to have to score something in the second half and we didn't manage to do that unfortunately.'

Schmidt admitted that he felt impotent for those final 90 seconds or so, from the moment New Zealand scrum-half Aaron Smith tapped the penalty until Crotty dotted down. Having sent messages onto the pitch via radio throughout the contest, now he had to sit back and wait, and hope.

'It's one of those times where to be honest you say nothing on the mic, you've got nothing to say because whatever will be will be,' he said. 'All you do is you watch and hope like any other supporter. You've just probably invested more time and effort in what happens. Did I feel that we could have defended it? Yeah. I don't think they did anything particularly special. Their pass quality was spot on, their handling was very, very good but we knew all those elements of their game prior to them arriving in Dublin. So for me those last 90 seconds they were just agonisingly slow. Even when Ryan Crotty did get over, we actually could have numbered up there and we didn't manage to. And possibly got him into touch but we didn't manage to. There were seven system errors in that 90 seconds, you know. I don't think there were too many missed tackles but some of those system errors were very minor and you wouldn't notice them, but there was a couple of fairly major system errors.'

Was this players losing trust in the team-mates inside them?

'Yeah – or making fatigued decisions,' said Schmidt. 'Vince Lombardi [legendary coach of the Green Bay Packers] said "Fatigue makes cowards of us all," but I think that is a really harsh way of saying it. I don't think anyone demonstrated any cowardice. I think there was a hell of a lot of courageous stuff that happened on Sunday but what fatigue does do is it limits our vision, it limits our processing. There's plenty of experiments that have been done where people are slower to react, reaction times drop off, decision making gets poorer with fatigue and that's part of what happened.

'But I was proud of their effort and I said so in the dressing room. I don't think that you can be critical when people have spent their last ounce of energy and being as generous with their bodies as they had been and then belittle that effort. So you say a few words of encouragement but does it make things any easier? Probably not. They desperately wanted to win that game and they wanted to keep the All Blacks out but a few decisions in that last 24-pass play weren't as good as the decisions that were being made when there was less pressure. We've got to learn from that and the way you learn from it is, having experienced that, getting a better clarity next time, having a better confidence next time in yourself and the trust of the players either side of you.'

All Blacks coach Steve Hansen had been quick to praise Ireland, of course. 'I think it's really important that you don't see this as a case of the All Blacks not having turned up today,' he said. 'The All Blacks turned up, but so did Ireland. We expect them to be tough, every time. But sometimes they don't believe they are as tough as they are.'

Schmidt didn't take much sustenance from his compatriot's words, but he was encouraged from the reaction he received from the Irish public in the days that followed. Defeat may have been painful but it was a launch pad for his team, just as it was the perfect starting point for this story.

'It's been a bloody tough few days,' Schmidt told us. 'But I would say the Irish public have been phenomenally supportive. A degree of that has been an unpleasant reminder of where we were and the opportunity that we had in both hands for 79 minutes of a game but a degree of it has also been uplifting. It's fantastic to have built some expectation. Now our challenge is to try and meet that expectation.'

Ireland: R Kearney; T Bowe, B O'Driscoll (L Fitzgerald 54), G D'Arcy, D Kearney; J Sexton (I Madigan 76), C Murray; C Healy (J McGrath 69), R Best (S Cronin 15), M Ross (D Fitzpatrick 66); D Toner (M McCarthy 66), P O'Connell (capt); P O'Mahony (K McLaughlin 57), S O'Brien, J Heaslip.

New Zealand: I Dagg (R Crotty 53); C Jane (B Barrett 67), B Smith, M Nonu, J Savea; A Cruden, A Smith; W Crockett (B Franks 61), A Hore (D Coles 43), C Faumuina (O Franks 57); B Retallick, S Whitelock; S Luatua (L Messam 57), R McCaw, K Read.

Referee: N Owens (Wales).

Scoring sequence: 4 mins: Murray try, Sexton con 7–0; 10 mins: Best try, Sexton con 14–0; 17 mins: R Kearney try 19–0; 25 mins: Savea try,

Cruden con 19–7; 33 mins: Sexton pen, 22–7; 52 mins: Cruden pen 22–10; 65 mins: B Franks try, Cruden con 22–17; 80+2 mins: Crotty try, Cruden con 22–24.

FRANCE 20, IRELAND 22
STADE DE FRANCE, 15 MARCH 2014

Less than five months after that heartbreaking defeat at the Aviva, Ireland somehow managed to find themselves in a remarkably similar end-game scenario, again with a massive prize at stake: a Six Nations title. This time they scraped through, but not without a heart-stopping scare – and palpitations weren't confined to the pitch. Another tight finish did nothing for the well-being of stressed reporters filing to an almost impossibly tight deadline.

The only positive aspect of a six o'clock kick-off on this, the final day of the 2014 Six Nations, was that everyone went into the game knowing exactly what Ireland required to win the title. While England had put 50 points on Italy in Rome earlier that afternoon, this wasn't enough to erase Ireland's advantage on points differential at the top of the table, with both teams having lost one game during the course of the championship. In other words, a win of any size would give Ireland their first title since 2009. Then there were your own professional requirements to consider. A late kick-off means filing your 900-word match report as early as possible, on or even before the final whistle, which means it's so much more convenient if the result is decided early, one way or the other. Somehow, you just knew things weren't going to be convenient on the evening in question. Hadn't Ireland and France drawn their previous two games in the Six Nations?

Besides, there was an almost unbearable pressure on Ireland to give Brian O'Driscoll the perfect send-off. The previous week at the Aviva, the team sponsors had got full value from a thumping 46–7 victory over Italy that was notable for the impact of the bench, which was responsible for three tries and the critical boost this gave to Ireland's points differential, but also for the after-match scenes, when the stadium stayed full for an entire 20 minutes after the final whistle as O'Driscoll received a special award for all he had contributed to Irish rugby. Having been robbed of the perfect send-off with the Lions the previous summer, he was now well placed to end his record-breaking international career on an ideal note, and in the ideal setting – remember, O'Driscoll had announced himself to the international game with a hat-trick in the Stade de France 14 years previously.

Just to make sure the players were aware of what was at stake, Joe Schmidt reminded them before the team bus left for the stadium. Schmidt recalled later: 'I said something like: "Lads, these are special days and you don't know how many special days you're going to get in a career, or in a lifetime. There's one guy in here who's not going to have a day like this again, so let's make sure this is a special day that he'll remember." I was standing next to him and I just tapped him on the shoulder and I saw him keep his head down a bit. And then I didn't know if I'd done the right thing. But if I hadn't done the right thing by him, I know I'd done the right thing by the other players because there's massive respect for him and they were going to make sure that whatever was required from them to do whatever they needed to do, that's the respect that he has amongst the group. They wanted to achieve something anyway but because it was supplemented by being Drico's last game, I think there was just a little more edge to it.'

It's rare that Schmidt presses emotional buttons like this before games, but he knew to prepare his players for an intense collision. Paris is a difficult enough venue for Irish teams – that victory in 2000 was the only time Ireland had won there in O'Driscoll's lifetime. Moreover, Schmidt knew that this French team was angry, having been walloped on home soil by the Welsh, having only sneaked past Scotland in Edinburgh in the penultimate round of matches and having taken heaps of abuse in the French media. Nicolas Mas, their gnarled old tight-head prop, had stormed out of one media conference days before the match because he didn't like the critical tone of certain questions.

Sure enough, Les Bleus gave Ireland a torrid start and built a 6–0 lead through two Maxime Machenaud penalties. Ireland responded with some of their best rugby of the championship, featuring significant contributions from the two players who'd come into the starting line-up since the New Zealand game: Chris Henry, who had replaced the injured Sean O'Brien, produced a sublime off-load to send Johnny Sexton over for Ireland's first try; and Andrew Trimble, who had deputised so effectively for Tommy Bowe that his peers would choose him as their Player of the Season, finished off some excellent approach work by O'Driscoll and Conor Murray. Sexton converted Trimble's try but was off target with a bread-and-butter penalty on the stroke of half-time – his third miss off the tee and a bizarre error from someone who was having a storming game in all other respects.

Ireland's fly-half scored his second try of the game – and his fourth in the space of eight days – shortly after the break. But France showed that they could keep counter-punching, with tries by Brice Dulin and Dimitri Szarzewski, even if the latter score looked highly questionable. The action replay showed that the French hooker had lost the ball forward at the critical moment, but for some reason, referee Steve Walsh decided that he didn't need to 'go upstairs' on this occasion. Surely Ireland weren't going to be on the wrong side of another season-defining refereeing decision?

Critically for them, they were blessed by luck in the final quarter, as Jean-Marc Doussain, France's half-back replacement, tugged another fairly straightforward penalty wide, allowing Ireland to remain two points ahead with 10 minutes remaining. In an improvement from the New Zealand game, they had scored 10 points after the break but once again found themselves in siege mode at the death, defending desperately as French coach Philippe Saint-André brought some heavy artillery off the bench. However, whereas the Kiwis' execution of basic skills had been flawless in the final seconds the previous November, France couldn't close the deal, despite working an overlap on the right-hand side of the pitch. The final pass, from Pascal Papé to Damien Chouly, clearly sailed forward by a foot or so.

But wait! Referee Walsh reckons this is worth reviewing. He asks TMO Gareth Simmonds to have a look at the replay. Was the forward pass actually a deflection off the hand of Dave Kearney, the last man in the Irish defensive line? Panic in pubs, clubs and living rooms all over Ireland and panic in Paris – especially in the press box. There are 72 seconds remaining when Walsh calls 'Time off' and asks for Simmonds' advice. Ever since the 52nd minute, when Sexton put Ireland 22–13 ahead, I've been hammering out a match report which is largely celebratory in tone. If Chouly's try is good, I've a whole lot of rewriting to do, and this is not a good time to be deleting text. Mercifully – for Ireland, for Irish supporters and for me – Walsh sees a clear forward pass on the video screen and utters six beautiful words: 'Forward pass mate, I've got it.'

Just over a minute later, the Irish players were embracing wildly on the pitch. Brian O'Driscoll struggled to hold back the tears as he was interviewed by RTÉ's Clare McNamara. A few minutes later, after the players had collected their medals and the fireworks flashed and the champagne corks popped, he looked altogether happier. As Schmidt said, 'So many world class sportsmen don't get to go out on their own terms. They kind of dwindle away rather than go out in a starburst. And he went out in an unbelievably positive fashion.'

Schmidt allowed himself a few celebratory drinks that night, but a few days later he was sitting before us hacks again, in debrief mode. How had the team progressed since New Zealand? Not perfectly – there had been one narrow defeat in Twickenham. But the level of performance had been consistently high, which was something new for an Irish international team. Typically, Schmidt said he'd been more fortunate than his predecessor, Declan Kidney, in so far as he'd been relatively untroubled by injuries and the team had been able to play their games in relatively kind conditions. There was still little doubt that Ireland were deserving Six Nations winners. 'Let's be accurate,' said an editorial in the French sports newspaper, L'Équipe. 'The best team – the most mature, the most balanced, the calmest, the best organised and by far – won this match and the tournament.'

Yes, they had relied on a little luck to get over the line – that missed penalty by Doussain and that forward pass by Papé – but Schmidt could see a team and a squad heading in the right direction.

'The forward pass? The fact that they created an overlap? The French just have some power carriers and sometimes we had to commit two or three guys to a tackle. That's what you're dealing with against France. But I thought Dave Kearney did incredibly well to close the space and effectively force an inaccurate pass. We had put ourselves under pressure with some loose kicks and that's something we'll keep working on. But the one thing I'd say is that in the New Zealand endgame we didn't get one thing right, and we got penalised. Then we made seven system errors in defence. This time we didn't have that domino effect of errors. There was a loose kick, or there was a defensive error, but other people stayed in the system and stayed accurate enough that we managed to keep them out.

'The frustrating thing is that we had control in both those games yet still finished on the back foot. In the All Blacks game we were leading so close to the finish that there will always be a massive disappointment no matter what happens in the future – for the players and the coaching staff and the whole wider management team. We were all pretty devastated that day. The fact that it didn't happen in France? Doussain kissed the kick. Sometimes those things fall your way and sometimes they don't.

'What's really probably satisfying for me is that they're two of the best teams in the world. Obviously the All Blacks are the elite. But the French, when they turn up and play like they did on Saturday – it gives us a little bit of quiet confidence that we're capable, when we are at our very best. We don't have someone like [Mathieu] Bastareaud who takes three tacklers to down him every time, or Billy Vunipola. We've got to be a better *team* than any other group of individuals who comes against us really. That's the way I'd summarise us.'

France: B Dulin; Y Huget, M Bastareaud, G Fickou (M Mermoz 76), M Médard; R Talès, M Machenaud (J-M Doussain 67); T Domingo (V Debaty h-t), D Szarzewski (G Guirado 69), N Mas (R Slimani 37); P Papé (capt), Y Maestri (A Flanquart 53); L Picamoles (S Vahaamahina 66), A Lapandry (W Lauret 66), D Chouly.

Ireland: R Kearney; A Trimble, B O'Driscoll, G D'Arcy (F McFadden

67), D Kearney; J Sexton (I Madigan 69), C Murray (E Reddan 64); C Healy (J McGrath 71), R Best (S Cronin 71), M Ross (M Moore 64); D Toner, P O'Connell (capt); P O'Mahony (I Henderson 64), C Henry, J Heaslip.

Referee: Steve Walsh (Australia).

Scoring sequence: 2 mins: Machenaud pen 3–0; 15 mins: Machenaud pen 6–0; 21 mins: Sexton try 6–5; 26 mins: Trimble try, Sexton con 6–12; 31 mins: Dulin try, Machenaud con 13–12; 45 mins: Sexton try, con 13–19; 53 mins: Sexton pen 13–22; 63 mins: Szarzewski try, Machenaud con 20–22.

IRELAND 26, AUSTRALIA 23
AVIVA STADIUM, 22 NOVEMBER 2014

By the end of 2014, Ireland were officially a better team than 12 months previously: third in the World Rugby rankings, as high as they'd ever been. Schmidt became visibly irritated when informed of this at a press conference the week before the Australia Test, as if such news could only increase expectation and thus increase pressure. Well, Ireland seemed to be handling pressure pretty well, having already beaten the second-ranked Springboks quite comfortably in their opening Test of the season, despite Schmidt having to carry out major surgery on his team, and his coaching staff – Simon Easterby, a stalwart for Ireland in the noughties, had taken over from John Plumtree as forwards coach.

With Sean O'Brien suffering from various physical ailments and Chris Henry recovering from a mini-stroke, Rhys Ruddock had slipped impressively into the number seven jersey against the Boks. Jack McGrath had also deputised well for Cian Healy, while Tommy Bowe and Simon Zebo were back on the wings. But of course the biggest surgical work was required in midfield, where O'Driscoll's retirement left a gaping wound. Robbie Henshaw and Jared Payne, a makeshift partnership, had exceeded expectations against South Africa, but Payne had picked up a niggle, so Henshaw moved to 13, to be partnered by Gordon D'Arcy, now on the final lap of a distinguished international career.

Ireland's final Test of 2014 was also a match-up between Schmidt and Michael Cheika, Leinster's two most recent and most successful coaches, as well as being the last time Ireland were scheduled to play a southern hemisphere team before the knock-out stages of the 2015 Rugby World Cup – assuming they get that far, of course. Speaking before the game, Schmidt knew the psychological benefits to be derived from a clean autumnal sweep, and the educational benefits also. 'No matter what happens against Australia, we'll definitely learn something about ourselves.'

As it turned out, they experienced something very similar to the New Zealand game of almost exactly 12 months before. Once again, they got off to a flyer, thanks to Zebo reading a perceptive and perfectly weighted kick by Sexton, and Bowe making an even better read under defensive pressure – from a position where the Wallabies looked like scoring in the left corner, Bowe's interception and 85-metre sprint had them trudging back to contemplate a 17-point deficit in the space of 17 minutes.

The problem was that this flurry of points created a spirit of freedom and openness in the Aviva, and if there's one opponent that thrives in this atmosphere, it's Australia. They duly thrived, scoring three tries before the break, two of them from deep inside their own half. That's three tries in the space of 19 minutes, when Ireland had conceded the grand total of four tries over the entire course of the 2014 Six Nations. That this second quarter avalanche had been precipitated by an errant Irish off-load prob- ably convinced Schmidt that a less risky attacking game was required for the coming months. Certainly they took fewer chances after the break here, kicking a lot of ball, though not necessarily kicking nearly as well as they had done earlier in the game.

Where Sexton was on the money was off the kicking tee. In the two big autumn Tests, he landed 13 from 14 shots at goal, including one nerve- less effort from 45 metres in the 63rd minute which was ultimately the winning of the match. Another hero was Mike Ross, who held things together during a couple of critical scrums deep in the Irish half, but in the final slug-fest, everyone in green was heroic. Cheika brought Quade Cooper, Kurtley Beale and Will Genia off the bench to speed up what had already been a breathless and brilliantly entertaining game, but Ireland's defence was at once disciplined and ferocious, epitomised by a blood- thirsty ball-and-all smash by Paul O'Connell on Australian number eight, Ben McCalman, as the Wallabies went for broke with ball in hand.

Australia may have played the more attractive, more expansive rugby, and afterwards Cheika made a point of mentioning Ireland's reliance on the high-ball game. But there could be no denying the benefits to Ireland's defensive game and their general self-belief of having held firm during that end-game against the least predictable and therefore most dangerous attacking side in the world. By a remarkable coincidence, the man who snuffed out the last Wallaby attack was Madigan, roughly 25 metres from the spot where he'd been left flapping 12 months previously as Ryan Crotty stole victory for the All Blacks. Instead of stunned silence, there was an incredible din at the Aviva when Madigan successfully competed on the deck and won the penalty for the final act of the game.

'It was very satisfying – to back up the South Africa win was the big thing,' said Ireland's man of the match and captain, Paul O'Connell. 'To beat South Africa the way we did, to pick them off accurately, was great, but this makes it all the more satisfying. It just wasn't a one-off win, to be able to keep our heads and close out the game was very satisfying.'

We barely heard from Schmidt post-match. The word was that he'd been suffering for the previous 24 hours from what he termed 'gut-ache' but which turned out to be appendicitis. After consulting with the team's medical staff, he was rushed to St Vincent's Hospital, a kilometre or two from the stadium. An uncomfortable time for him, but at least the day after he woke to the realisation that Ireland had won nine of their 10 Tests in 2014, giving themselves the perfect launch pad in the process.

Ireland: R Kearney (F Jones 78); T Bowe, R Henshaw, G D'Arcy (I Madigan 59), S Zebo; J Sexton (E Reddan 78), C Murray (Reddan 71–76); J McGrath, R Best (S Cronin 68), M Ross; D Toner (D Foley 62), P O'Connell (capt); P O'Mahony, R Ruddock, J Heaslip.

Australia: I Folau; A Ashley-Cooper, T Kuridrani (K Beale 46), M Toomua (Brumbies), H Speight (Brumbies); B Foley (Q Cooper 65), N Phipps (W Genia 68); J Slipper (B Robinson 76), S Fainga'a (J Hanson 71), S Kepu (T Faulkner 71); S Carter (W Skelton 72), R Simmons; L Jones (J Schatz 54), M Hooper (capt), B McCalman.

Referee: Glen Jackson (New Zealand).

Scoring sequence: 6 mins: Sexton pen 3–0; 12 mins: Zebo try, Sexton con 10–0; 14 mins: Bowe try, Sexton con 17–0; 18 mins: Phipps try, Foley con 17–7; 23 mins: Foley try 17–12; 31 mins: Phipps try 17–17; 37 mins: Foley pen 17–20; 40+3 mins: Sexton pen 20–20; 46 mins: Sexton pen 23–20; 49 mins: Foley pen 23–23; 64 mins: Sexton pen 26–23.

3

CALM BEFORE THE STORM: NORA STAPLETON

Kate Rowan

The best way to introduce Ireland's out-half, Nora Stapleton, is with an anecdote from her childhood in Fahan, on Donegal's Inishowen Peninsula: 'When I was about four years of age my mother tried to force me into a dress and sat me in mass in it. She said I sat for the whole duration of mass with a sour puss on my face. Then I went home, I went upstairs and cut up my dress with a pair of scissors. Since then she has said, "Do what you do." I love wearing dresses now, but at that time I was stubborn – it was not what I wanted.

'From the time I could walk I was an active child. I would climb the highest tree in the garden when I was three, and my mother spent my whole childhood worrying about me, but she realised there was no point in worrying because I was going to do whatever I wanted to do.' A headstrong child may drive a parent round the bend, but sometimes this obstinacy will become an unyielding determination that will take the young person on a journey towards something special.

The members of Ireland's 2015 Six Nations women's squad that I interviewed, although very different characters, shared an unstinting tenacity. Stapleton was not the first player I interviewed for this book, but she was the first member of the squad I had become acquainted with. Last year I was involved in helping the IRFU to organise and provide coverage of domestic women's rugby at interprovincial and club levels. The idea was to try to get weekly round-ups of these games in as many of the national newspapers and online media outlets as possible, in an attempt to build on the curiosity sparked by the 2013 Six Nations grand slam and the 2014 run in the Rugby World Cup. Although at this point I had experience of covering women's rugby at international level, there had not been much demand for coverage of the domestic game, so I needed to do my research before my assignment began. I was introduced to Stapleton in her capacity as Women's and Girls' Development Executive for the IRFU, and although I only dealt with her via email and telephone, her passion and enthusiasm for growing the women's game was infectious. I wondered how it would translate to Stapleton the rugby player. In the back of my mind this sparked an idea: that if I ever had the chance, I would very much like to write a feature article about her. So, when planning this book, I decided that Stapleton would be one of the players from whose perspective the story of the 2015 Six Nations campaign would be told. Her 'day job' in helping to develop her sport would lend itself well to this, as she could provide insights into how women's rugby had changed in the past few seasons.

When one is speaking to her, that steely determination forged during her tomboy years growing up is very apparent, as is a searing honesty on a wide range of topics, from her self-doubts to why coaching women can be very different to coaching men. She kicks off her telling of the transition from Philip 'Goose' Doyle's part-time management team to the Tom Tierney-led full-time professional set-up: 'When we came back from the World Cup and all the management stepped away, I know there was some negative publicity about [why] there hasn't been any management team put in place yet, and from the players' point of view.' As for a potential conflict of interest because she is an employee of the IRFU: 'Maybe it was a little bit different for me. I was trying not to wear my work or player hat. Not that it is hard to move between the two, but I would have had the players giving out to me – "Why have we not got new management?" – and I am saying, "Well, there is no rush. It was no different in previous years." We never do our first camp until the first weekend after Christmas.

It was the exact same last year. Yes, if you have any queries on training, it's nice to pick up the phone and ask somebody, and we didn't have that, but the whole thing was "How do we put it into high performance?" When the management did come in, Tom is a great guy. Nothing against previous management, but they just brought something new.' There is no disrespect towards the old regime, just pragmatism in terms of the team's future success. In order for Ireland to reach the levels of the likes of England, a full-time professional coaching structure is imperative.

It appeared before the tournament that Ireland's women's season would be a transitional phase due to a number of high-profile retirements, including that of captain Fiona Coghlan, and the bedding in of the new management structure, and coming under the IRFU's High Performance Unit for the first time. In the squad of 30 players, 12 were uncapped. Along with Stapleton, veterans of past seasons such as Niamh Briggs (who would be named captain), Sophie Spence, Marie Louise Reilly, Jenny Murphy and Tania Rosser returned to the fold along with fresh faces such as sevens players Katie Fitzhenry, Hannah Tyrrell and Aoife Doyle. As a result of such sweeping change, according to the then 31-year-old Stapleton, 'Nobody gave us much hope coming into this Six Nations, and we achieved beyond what a lot of people thought we would achieve.'

Although Stapleton's life now seems to be dominated by the oval ball, and playing at amateur level for her club Old Belvedere, her adopted province Leinster and Ireland, this was not always the case. During her youth she dipped into whatever sports were available around her home parish in Fahan and in the neighbouring town of Buncrana – everything from Gaelic football to handball to basketball and soccer. Neither her mother Siobhan nor father Jim had a particular passion for sport. However, her maternal grandmother Iris Grant, who had been a keen hockey and camogie player in her youth, was both her granddaughter's biggest fan and harshest critic in her early sporting pursuits. After Stapleton received a soccer scholarship while studying at University College Dublin, her UCD team qualified for the early rounds of UEFA's women's club competitions and as a result travelled to France, Norway and Croatia for matches. Granny Iris would organise her holidays from the family business – Grant's shoe shop in Buncrana, which Siobhan now runs – to attend her granddaughter's away fixtures. This support continued as Stapleton crossed codes from playing inter-county football for Donegal to playing rugby for Ireland, and Iris attended the 2014 World Cup in Paris.

An irony in Stapleton's sporting story is that the one sport she could not dabble in as a child was rugby. As a youngster she was bitterly disappointed when her best friend Kieran O'Gorman joined the local rugby club and she could not follow, as girls were not allowed. Having drifted apart as they grew up, as fate would have it the two old pals now both play for Old Belvedere. O'Gorman was capped earlier this year for Ireland's Club XV. Stapleton recalls O'Gorman laughingly commenting on how, despite everything, she had beaten him to it in playing for Ireland.

Stapleton does not shy away from addressing the very different environments of men's and women's rugby in Ireland: 'At my own club, Old Belvedere, we have had to fight. It was difficult at the start where we didn't exist. We were separate entities playing with the Belvo name. Now our membership has grown so much that the club have realised [it needs] to embrace this. That is what I would say to all clubs. They need to embrace women's rugby.' Up to the 1970s, membership of Old Belvedere was reserved for old boys of Dublin's Belvedere College. Stapleton describes how the old school ties, which are such an integral part of men's rugby in Ireland, are non-existent in the women's game, and how this struck her when attending a function at Old Belvedere. 'Rugby is all school linked. I didn't know how important schools were but it's as a real eye opener. It was like a man's cult or something. It was the first time women were ever invited. It was because we had done so well in the World Cup and the Six Nations and they felt it was right to invite the girls. It was full of men, all the alickadoos, all the Presidents with their chains around their necks. I was talking to one and he said from the first one in November, they spend every Friday going from one school dinner to another school dinner. Women's rugby isn't like that at all. It is coming from something completely different. It is your community, your club, your friends and it is where you want to hang out.'

Another difference Stapleton has noticed between the men's and women's games is in how players wish to communicate with their coaches, coming from her experience in rugby but also from working for six years as a development officer with the GAA, dedicated to the coaching of youngsters: 'If I'm told to do something, I like to understand why we are doing it, so I can paint that picture in my mind and it becomes a genuine reason, as opposed to just "Do this." Just explain to me. And I'm taking this from coaches and coaching myself. If I tell a young lad to run through a brick wall they will, where the girl will say "Why do you want me to run through it, can I not run over this? Would it not make more sense?" It is not that we think the coach is right or wrong, but it's about building a depth of understanding.' She continues, in relation to the beginning of Tierney's tenure: 'Tom is coming to us and we are adults, but we are adults still building our rugby knowledge, so he has to be aware of that, while we are trying to absorb as much as possible. Even knowing the rules – I probably don't know all the rules at this stage. There are so many you forget some of them. What young boys would learn when they are 15, we are only learning. I am a good bit down that road now, but that is a big thing.'

When recounting previous Test matches, Stapleton brought up an issue that had once caused her performance to deteriorate. An issue that no male athlete will ever face: the dreaded 'time of the month'. As a woman, this was a topic that immediately piqued my interest, as it is not frequently discussed in relation to women's sport. As Stapleton explains, it can create havoc: 'For me, it really affects my sport. No matter how many pills or painkillers you take, it affects me mentally, so my decision-making drops right down. I take iron tablets, vitamin C, vitamin B, vitamin everything. It still affects me.'

I mentioned in passing to a male colleague that a woman's natural hormonal fluctuations can impact performance. He was not joking when he remarked: 'If you put too much of that *Sex and the City* stuff in about periods, no one will take you or women's rugby seriously!' Why shouldn't we discuss an issue that affects half the population? If we really want to understand women in sport we need to look at the reality of being a female athlete.

Whether they play sport or not, most women can empathise with how as a fly-half Stapleton needs to have razor-sharp decision-making skills, but these can decline starkly for a few days each month. 'It's all about decision making, and my decision making slows right down and it's blurred. You are really fatigued. If you are fatigued, you are mentally not as sharp as you need to be. That is what I find. I can't make a proper decision.' Many women will also agree that sometimes, when a group of females are all feeling somewhat hormonal, it can lead to tension. There is a hint of dark humour when Stapleton remarks that 'There are times if everybody is synced, that a training session is going to be awful – too many bitches! I'd say the management noticed it. I think one training session we all came off the pitch and it could have been a captain's run and everyone was at each other. We were dropping every single ball and I remember the management looking around and I was thinking, "They don't really know what is going on." I think it turned out that about 10 of us …' With a sardonic chuckle she concludes, 'We will put that training session down to that.'

Returning to the early build-up to the Six Nations and the arrival of Tierney and his assistants Declan O'Brien and Derek Dowling, Stapleton's description helps to shed light on a player's mindset: 'The first few sessions were weird. It was like every player was in for themselves, trying to establish themselves. You are obviously a little bit nervous. You want to get picked and this, that and another. There was no captain, so there was a lack of leadership and everybody thinking they were the leaders and it was just a crazy time. We all couldn't wait for it to settle and get on with business. Tom and Deccie came in. Analysis came in. Everything was in place. They ticked all the right boxes. They were doing things the right way and it was going to take time.' What was different in training between 2015 and previous seasons? 'Maybe there was another level of professionalism brought to it and a better understanding of the game. Even down to simple things like game management. Whereas before we would have thought, we don't have much of the ball, we are going to have to hold onto the ball no matter where we are on the pitch. When actually, why would you hold onto the ball inside our 22 just because we hadn't touched it? Little things like that, being given the freedom to actually execute those game plans a little bit better. We need to improve our skills but I thought we did the basics well.'

Members of the public often have a fascination with what one would describe as 'sport's sufferers'. For players such as Roy Keane, regardless of the success they achieve, they are crippled by a constant fear of their performance dipping that feeds into their determination to keep improving.

Covering rugby, I have developed a particular interest in the game's 'suf-ferers'. The two most prominent are World Cup winners and icons. Eng-land's Jonny Wilkinson has spoken openly about how in his striving for perfection he has encountered issues with depression and anxiety. New Zealand's Richie McCaw has spoken of how, despite the adoration of a nation, he could not enjoy the immediate aftermath of the All Blacks' 2011 World Cup win on home soil. Not only had he played on a broken foot, but such was the pressure he was under as captain to return the Webb Ellis Cup to rugby's spiritual home, after a 24-year absence, that all he could feel was a mixture of exhaustion and relief rather than ela-tion. Stapleton too may have those 'sufferer' tendencies in her personality: 'People would say to me "It must be great playing for Ireland during the Six Nations." I spend those three months worrying I might not get on the team, and then when I finish each match I am worried about what I did wrong, then you are worried again you won't get picked for the next game. It is just a constant high and low. The only time you can relax is when you put on the jersey and you are walking onto the pitch. You know "I am safe now, I am playing."'

This raw honesty is demonstrated again when she speaks of the need to retain both 'mental confidence and self-confidence'. She shakes her head with regret, and says: 'I definitely don't have enough of those I admire, people who just ooze confidence. I look at them and see they know they are going to get picked by the way they talk and act, and I would struggle with that.' Does this self-doubt help to drive her performance? 'It makes you hungry but at the same time it holds you back. I over-analyse everything, and at 10 you have to make quick decisions. I am always trying to make the perfect decision where there is no such thing. Even a decision that is 80% correct is a half-decent decision. Sometimes it might slow you up and instead of having a crack and taking the ball on, I might pass it out. Instead of putting a chip or grubber through I think, "No, I might get given out to about that", and I hold on to the ball.'

Stapleton outlines how she prepares for the accurate decision-making she so desperately craves: 'I have a whiteboard at home and I draw up mini-pitches and ... it just has scrums in different places of the pitch and maybe what I do off those scrums – how I defend or attack them. You do the same for lineouts. You just keep drawing up scenarios and try to answer them in your own head. When I was first learning how to play I used to draw up all the moves and stick them up on my bedroom wall, so before I was falling asleep at night, you end up reading them, you wake up in the morning, you end up reading them.' This must take its toll on relationships? When she mentions her girlfriend, rather than asking about how her girlfriend supports her, I can't help but enquire a little hesitantly regarding her sexuality, mainly due to the fact that there are no 'out' role models in Irish rugby.

Stapleton's response shows the sort of approach we should be taking regarding sports stars' sexuality: that it should not be seen as a big deal. 'I don't really want to do that because why should that have anything to do with anything? I admire people who come out publicly but I don't necessarily want to do the whole "I am a gay rugby player and this is great" – I don't know if there is a need for it, if people really want to know that about me – you could spend five minutes on Google and you would probably find that out. I don't think different sports need that either … there are gay women represented in every single sport; that is how common it is. I just think "This is me" and I am sure there will be people who will read this and won't have known that I was gay. But I am not going to be on the Irish team forever either, so once you come out and do all that, you might not get picked for the next match. Maybe there was one time where I thought "Maybe I should do that?", but definitely not – all I want is to keep playing, keep improving as much as I can and get a couple more caps to my name.'

This is very much in line with how many in Ireland hope that attitudes around sexuality will evolve in the aftermath of the Marriage Referendum. It is a far cry from when Stapleton was a teen: 'When I was 14, 15, 16, I would have had feelings for girls and not understood why, or I used to look up magazines' problem pages to see if any of those letters in there would highlight for me, "You are not gay, this is just a phase" or "You are." I don't remember there being any kind of support or information that could have explained anything to me, available to me as a teenager.' She believes that 'Because of the referendum, you are going to see gay marriages … as part of society. That will help young people growing up, that they will never have to go through that kind of confusion.'

The most empowering thing to do is to get back on track and talk about

Stapleton's girlfriend of three years, Claire, and how the boyfriends and girlfriends of Ireland's women players support their other halves: 'Claire is amazing, she helps me through all those highs and lows I do get from playing. When we started going out together, our first Six Nations together probably would have been a lot harder than what it is now, because for me rugby is all-consuming. I would have been mental! That would have been quite difficult. It is difficult for her too because she sees the highs and the lows I go through. As we go through more matches, more Six Nations and tournaments, we are learning a lot. I learn to control rugby so it doesn't seep into [me] when [I] get home from training. It is the same kind of thing as you don't want to bring work home with you.'

For Nora Stapleton, the 2015 Six Nations would involve that yearly journey through agony and ecstasy, fuelled by her and her teammates' unwavering resolve.

4

MAN WITH A PLAN: JOE SCHMIDT

Peter O'Reilly

The news that Schmidt had been taken to hospital came as something of a shock to everyone. Up until that point, he had seemed bulletproof and a symbol for consistent success: four trophies in the space of three years in charge at Leinster, and now a Six Nations title at his first attempt, and this in an even-numbered year – traditionally more difficult than the odd-numbered ones, as there are fixtures in London and Paris. Some, including this letter-writer to the *Irish Independent*, believed Schmidt's talents should be put to an even greater good.

Sir,

I would just like to say thank you to Joe Schmidt for what he has done for Irish rugby. I would like to wish him a speedy recovery too, and would like ask if, when the World Cup is over, would he be prepared to run for Taoiseach?

T G Gavin, Dalkey, Co Dublin

It's amusing now to look back and recall how some in the French media had questioned Schmidt's credentials as a head coach, given that he had been the mild-mannered assistant to Vern Cotter at Clermont Auvergne. These weren't the only doubters. Even Johnny Sexton, now perceived as Schmidt's main representative on the pitch with Ireland and a self-confessed admirer of the coach, wondered aloud about Schmidt's temperament before his appointment by Leinster. After Sexton and Leo Cullen had spent some time in Schmidt's company, Sexton voiced his solitary concern about their prospective new coach: Was he too nice a bloke to be in charge of a club with designs on dominating European rugby? Cullen reasoned that if Schmidt had been capable of maintaining discipline as deputy principal at a secondary school of 1600 boys (Tauranga Boys High School – Cullen had done his homework), then he'd be able to manage 50-odd professional athletes.

The Leinster players found out pretty quickly that their new boss was perfectly well equipped to be just that – the boss. His video review sessions became famous for a few reasons. First, the players could see that Schmidt had a technical knowledge of the game that was second to none. Even a scrummaging nerd like Mike Ross saw that he had a sharp understanding of the complexities of the scrum as well as an insight into the habits and scrummaging preferences of most of the props on the professional circuit. And this was a former wing. Second, just as Schmidt was quick to praise anything that someone had done accurately, no one was immune to criticism. That message became clear at the meeting when he picked Brian O'Driscoll up for some rare error. If your best player is being kept on his toes, this not only sends out a message of egalitarianism, but also sets a high standard.

Jono Gibbes was Schmidt's forwards coach for his three years at Leinster and he saw how players became more personally accountable for the team ethic. Gibbes described how things worked to the *Irish Times*: 'Jamie Heaslip put it pretty well once when we played Bath at the Rec and the ball got kicked long down the field. He was absolutely buggered but he just started running because all he could think was: "I'm not going to be pulled apart on Monday." Stories about those review sessions have since grown legs. Certainly by the time [Schmidt] was at the end with Leinster he didn't even have to say anything on Monday. The players could see the footage and know exactly what he was going to say and pipe up. But I think one of the reasons why the Monday sessions are so ruthless is because he drives teamwork. You're either working your socks off for someone or you're getting off the ground and getting back up to work, because it's a game for teamwork. You rely on each other.

Okay, there are individuals that change the course of a game but it's the collective strength of the group which is the main thing. I don't think he ever personalised something on a Monday session, but that's not to say he wasn't harsh. But he was only harsh because the individual may have affected the performance of the other players, and that was the point he was making. Joe's smart, he's got a good way about him, but he doesn't accept people letting their teammates down.'

In an early Leinster team meeting, Schmidt asked the players to come up with the three adjectives that they'd like to describe the team. He then applied the qualities so rigorously that they came to define them. They define any team Schmidt coaches and they define the man himself.

DISCIPLINED

Schmidt was only a couple of months in Ireland the first time I sat down to interview him one-on-one at Leinster's old training base in Riverview, but already his near-obsession with punctuality had been established. Peter Breen, the press officer, politely suggested that my turning up five minutes ahead of the appointed time would be no harm; Schmidt would definitely be there a few minutes early himself. If the coach was so atten-tive to detail in his dealings with the media, you can imagine what he's like with his team. Poor time-keeping simply isn't acceptable. If the meet-ing is scheduled for 10 o'clock, in Joe's world, you're expected to be there for 9.55. During Ireland's short tour to Argentina in the summer of 2014, some meetings actually started eight minutes ahead of schedule. 'We were so punctual, it actually became funny,' Paul O'Connell recalled. 'Joe saw the funny side of it, too.' Perhaps, but he wouldn't see the funny side of anyone being eight minutes late. At Leinster, one player lost his place in a Heineken Cup team as a result of not turning up on time. If there's one thing that focuses a player's attention, it's the prospect of not being picked to play.

Schmidt's theory on time-keeping is that it sets the tone for everything, including how a team performs on the pitch. He accepts that no rugby team is capable of being spotlessly law-abiding on the pitch while still remaining ultra-competitive. Rugby just doesn't work that way. But with Leinster and Ireland, he aims to keep penalty concessions to single figures per match by maintaining a high quality of technical execution in the danger areas of the field – specifically in the tackle zone/breakdown. Accordingly, Leinster won the Pro-12 Fair Play award under Schmidt's stewardship, while in the two Six Nations championships when he's been in charge, Ireland have conceded fewest penalties and received just one yellow card in 10 games.

Schmidt can accept that players make mistakes. What he can't abide is someone not knowing their role in any given play. When he made Leinster the most lethal attacking side in Europe, much was made of the improvement he had brought about in their passing game, and it's true that he put pressure on players to improve the technical excellence of their distribution off both hands, and in every type of pass. But for Schmidt's 'power plays' to work as well as he intends them to work requires accuracy from every moving part, and that means players who may not touch the ball once during the attacking sequence. It could be a prop cleaning out the left-hand side of the second ruck in the sequence, maybe a minor obstruction on one of the opposition's pillar defenders, and this could make or break the play.

'What we noticed immediately about him was his knowledge of the opposition and the detail he'll go into to ensure a move works,' wrote Johnny Sexton in *Becoming a Lion*. 'There are times when you might think you have the line-break executed to perfection but he'll insist that it's not precise enough to break the team we're up against next. So we go back and do it again. How many times? Until we get it right. Just when you think we've nailed it, he spots that the blind-side winger wasn't "animating", or drawing attention to himself, the way Joe wanted. No one is allowed to be redundant. If you're not actively involved in the play, he wants you doing something to make the opposition think that you are. I love that attention to detail.'

For Conor Murray, it's also the level of detail that Schmidt seeks which sets him apart. 'He's amazing,' says Murray. 'He's definitely helped me become a better player. No matter who you're playing, he instils a belief that you can win the game if you do what he tells you to do. You get your role, 14 others the same, and if we all do our jobs, we will all be in the game in the last 10 minutes. He will have gone through the opposition, every strength and every weakness, and you end up with a conviction that winning is attainable. I realise Joe isn't going to be with Ireland forever and I want to enjoy every season I work with him.'

At Leinster, Schmidt had the luxury of access to his players, certainly for more time than he gets as Ireland coach. It's a numbers game. Ireland play 10 or 12 games a year; Leinster could play 30. As national coach, he has to make full use of that access, so he places severe pressure on his players to be ready for the time that they spend together. If he introduces a new series of moves while they're together in November, he'll expect every detail of those plays to be known 'off by heart' when the squad reassembles for a couple of days at Christmas or when they meet again at the end of January to prepare for the Six Nations. There are no hand-outs or 'play-books', which are routine in other set-ups. The information is posted in the team room and there is a limited time for players to absorb and memorise it. From what we hear, players undergo the sort of stress they haven't experienced since their final school examinations.

But this attention to detail works. We saw Schmidt's precision at its most laser-like against Biarritz in an Amlin Cup semi-final a couple of years ago, when Leinster had three attacking platforms in the course of the first half and scored tries on all of them. 'One of the things that gives players confidence is when things work,' Schmidt reasons. 'A lot of our strong position or scoring comes from things that are rehearsed on the training field. Players get confidence from that and buy into it. That confidence allows them to have some clarity in their role that hopefully makes us a little bit more cohesive as a unit.'

Ireland's game-plan is prescriptive, highly structured and highly disciplined. It is also successful. No one is complaining.

HUMBLE

Schmidt didn't have to preach this quality to Leinster when he arrived in Ireland in the summer of 2010. The players were aware that they were perceived as being a little precious. They needed to take themselves a little less seriously, to connect more with their supporters. They couldn't have chosen a better guide towards humility than Schmidt. He understands the value of openness, of giving people time. He has the common touch. At an early training session hosted by his old club Mullingar, the Leinster players noticed how he seemed to know all the old-timers' names, even though it was a couple of decades since he'd played there on what the Kiwis call their OE, or overseas experience. Even now, as Ireland coach, he does an inordinate number of speaking engagements for clubs and schools, when time permits. He always speaks without notes, is always entertaining, and never accepts a fee. If the club insists, he will redirect the fee towards a charity of his choice, such as Epilepsy Ireland – Luke, the youngest of Joe and Kellie's four children, suffers from epilepsy.

Working as a rugby coach means Schmidt is well travelled, but he has described himself as 'a small-town kid'. That small town was Woodville, not far from Palmerston North in New Zealand's North Island, and home to no more than 1,600 people. The details of his upbringing will resonate with anyone remotely familiar with the game in that country. As Schmidt recalled in one of our interviews: 'My dad [David Schmidt] was a huge rugby fan, mad keen. He was down at the local club on Saturday mornings when I started playing at five or six, sometimes reffing, sometimes coaching. I remember him taking me to see the Manawatu team that held the Ranfurly Shield in 1976. It was a pretty tough game against Wanganui. The exciting thing was that the 10 for Manawatu, Brian Morris, was a student teacher at Woodville Primary at the time. Actually knowing one of the players – that was a big thrill.'

In time, Schmidt would play provincial rugby himself, and the highlight of his playing career was to be part of the Manawatu team that came close to beating the touring French side in 1989. Viewers of RTÉ TV even got to see Schmidt score a try in that game, courtesy of the researchers on the *Second Captains* programme. The clip shows a slight, blond and energetic wing, racing past Jean-Baptiste Lafond to get first touch on a cross-kick. With typical modesty, and with the critical eye of a coach, Schmidt says: 'Poor defending by Lafond. If he'd positioned himself correctly, I would never have got close.'

RELENTLESS

When Leinster chose this adjective as an ideal description for themselves, they surely had in mind the periods of pressure when they hammered away at opponents for intense stretches of attack: perfectly choreographed, rigorously executed. But it's also a good work to describe Schmidt's own working practices and his quest for perfection. And to think that he believed the international schedule, with all its fallow periods, would give him more time for family and relaxation! If anything, he has become even more wrapped up in his job.

'I'm always doubting what we are doing and I'm always trying to solve things,' he said after the 2014 Six Nations. 'I might be looking at problems that haven't existed yet but I'll be thinking: If we do x next time and they counter with y, how do we get to z? In other words, I'd better try to get a solution to that problem before it becomes a problem at all. I think sometimes I should apologise to my wife. I'm hard to live with. There's times that I just don't come to bed for a long time because I'll be sitting there with six or seven bits of paper with potential solutions scrawled all over them. Without being an amateur psychologist about it, I'm always trying to prove that I can do the job because I always doubt that I can.'

Schmidt pays tribute to his coaching team and his support staff – highly regarded specialists like Les Kiss (defence), Simon Easterby (forwards), Greg Feek (scrum), Richie Murphy (kicking), Jason Cowman (fitness), Mervyn Murphy (video analysis) and others. But he is a control freak because that's what his position requires. So while he delegates, he'll still be on top of everything, to the extent that there are times when he appears capable of going without sleep. During the countdown to the Six Nations opener in Rome, preparations were jeopardised by a cold snap, which affected the training pitches at Carton House. Met Éireann predicted a slight increase in temperature, but Schmidt needed to know if the pitches would be playable. He rose at 4 a.m. to see if they'd take a stud, then again at 5 a.m. and 6 a.m. While the players were tucked up asleep, their coach was out there in the frozen darkness, taking care of business.

Occasionally coaches from other sports will ask to attend training sessions, searching for the 'one percenters' that might give them an edge. Schmidt is open to the cross-pollination of ideas from sport to sport, and is just as much of a magpie himself. One of his guests in 2014 was Mick Malthouse, the legendary Aussie Rules coach, and Schmidt loved picking his brains about match-day preparation, player management and the like. When Schmidt asked how Malthouse had maintained his enthusiasm for his job over so many years, the Aussie told him the secret was to work long hours but never to take your work home with you. 'I'd be different to that,' said Schmidt, unapologetically. 'I take my work pretty much wherever I go. Players need that balance, they have to freshen and regenerate, but I don't think it's necessary for coaches.'

Schmidt does have an interest in other sports. Like so many Kiwis, he keeps an eye on the gee-gees, and he found time to attend the 2015 Cricket World Cup final between Australia and New Zealand. He takes an interest in Gaelic games and once even delayed a training session in Carton so that everyone could watch the climax of the All Ireland Hurling Final from Croke Park. He's also a keen reader who has written book reviews for an Irish newspaper. But when he's working, he's full on. The only time he really steps back is when it's getting close to kick-off and the players need to generate some more primal energy in the dressing room. It's rarely that he will tap any emotional buttons.

'Not really,' he said after the 2014 Six Nations success. 'I'm a bit of a one-trick pony. I've only got what I have got. I'm not good at the emotional thing. Paul O'Connell is an inspirational character. When he speaks, people listen. When he speaks, it is genuinely from the heart and he's a hell of a lot better at emotionally charging people. I'm more about making sure that you're lucid, that your decision-making is good. If you play purely on emotion, you can very quickly get yourself into trouble. I think it's incredibly important to be really lucid. One of the things that can contribute to inconsistent performance is being overly aroused – one day, your performance is super but the next, someone picks up a yellow card and then you're on the back foot.'

Accordingly, Schmidt wasn't rattling any sabres when he met with a small group of Sunday newspaper journos before the 2015 Six Nations. His main preoccupation seemed to be with managing public expectations – that November clean sweep had served to land Ireland the favourites' tag. Schmidt seemed more exercised by the mildly critical commentary about Ireland's low-risk game-plan, though he conceded there were areas for improvement.

'Even though you'd have to be delighted with those three results, there were facets of our game that took the gloss off a little bit,' he said. 'I know that we finished the Australia game with some great defensive sets but we conceded three tries in that game. We can't afford that. Some of our set-piece stuff wasn't as good as we would have liked it to have been, but there were some real positives in that we found a way to win even if elements of our game weren't going great.

'We're going to have to cope with an expectation that we should win in Rome. We put that expectation on ourselves. We know it's very hard to win a Six Nations if you lose your first game. At the same time, we needed a late drop-goal to win in Rome in 2011 and we lost 22–15 over there two years ago. You match our back row against theirs and is there a lot in it? Or the front rows? Even the second row? Who was the top tackler in last year's Six Nations?'

Turns out it was Quintin Geldenhuys, Italy's South African-born lock. How do we know? Because Joe told us so.

5

ITALY: HANNAH TYRRELL

Kate Rowan

Born in 1990, Hannah Tyrrell missed the magic and hype of the Republic of Ireland's Italia '90 odyssey to the World Cup quarter-finals, but some of her earliest memories are from Jackie's Army's assault on USA '94, and like many of her generation she was raised on and inspired by this legacy. As a result, she spent much of her childhood chasing a soccer ball close to her home in Clondalkin. Growing up as the only girl on her football team, she dreamt of emulating Manchester United stars such as David Beckham, Paul Scholes, Ryan Giggs and, of course, our very own Roy Keane. Most kids realise at some point that they will never grace Old Trafford's Theatre of Dreams; for Tyrrell this moment came at the age of 12 when she had to leave her soccer team, regardless of talent or ability, as boys and girls were segregated.

Of course she was initially disappointed: 'It was very hard as I had always played with the boys' team. It was hard not to play anymore with your friends who you had grown up with. Obviously, playing with your best friends is great, but of course there is a reason for it as boys get stronger and faster than the girls.' Unfortunately for young Tyrrell, there wasn't a *Bend It Like Beckham* style all-girls team in her corner of Dublin at that time; thus began her journey as something of a code-hopper. She continued to kick round balls, but now they were Gaelic footballs with her local club, Round Towers. Soon after this conversion she was included in Dublin's under-14s panel, beginning over a decade's involvement at inter-country level, through under-16s and minors to seniors, winning a number of All-Ireland titles with the Dubs along the way.

One compelling aspect of the 24-year-old's story is that just over two years ago, as her current Ireland colleagues such as Niamh Briggs and Nora Stapleton were on the cusp of winning Ireland's historic Six Nations Women's grand slam, she was yet to pick up a rugby ball. She describes rugby as being 'all the rage' at that time; former Ireland international Sharon 'Chopper' Lynch encouraged her to try it at Old Belvedere. Lynch could see Tyrrell's potential for sevens rugby: the IRFU were on the hunt for fresh talent in Ireland's bid to qualify for the 2016 Rio Olympics. For Tyrrell, one could say, the rest is history.

In May 2014 she had to stop playing for the Dubs mid-league season when rugby gave her the opportunity to become a full-time athlete: she was asked to join the IRFU's centralised sevens programme, which, unlike women's fifteens, has a structure where the women train as professionals. She quickly established herself as a force to be reckoned with in the short form of the game, and leapt at an opportunity for sevens players to also become involved in fifteens, impressing the coaches in a trial. She would make her debut on the right wing in Ireland's Six Nations opener against Italy in Florence.

It may be heading towards hyperbole to describe Tyrrell as Irish women's sport's equivalent of Australian code-hopping superstar *du jour* Israel Folau, who segued from rugby league to Aussie rules to rugby union, where he has dazzled for the Wallabies since making his debut against the British and Irish Lions in 2013. A comparison that may make the down-to-earth Tyrrell blush, but her story so far certainly casts her as something of a sporting Superwoman. Yet her athletic CV only scratches the surface of what a remarkable character she is.

During the Six Nations, I interviewed Tyrrell over the phone for a magazine feature. She discussed her varied sporting career, her ambition and drive, and how she was balancing studying history and geography in UCD with being a professional athlete. She even gave me a bit of a history lesson on the causes of the First World War, while humbly batting off praise concerning her recent form. She came across as the sort of girl who just seemed to have life sussed. The girl with whom you would share a college tutorial group and envy her ability to make multi-tasking seem so easy: 'Look at Hannah playing two types of rugby for Ireland and she really knows her stuff for this course, while I can barely make the deadlines for assignments and get to my 9 a.m. lectures on time!'

Appearances, however, can be deceptive. In researching this book, I had arranged to meet Tyrrell in a café in Donnybrook. Despite still being in recovery from a dislocated shoulder picked up in the final match of the tournament against Scotland, she looked the very picture of health: tall, slim and confident. There was a glow to her skin that seems reserved for elite-level athletes. After discussing her Gaelic football career in detail, I decided to ask her to fill me in a little on her academic and work background. She began by telling me that before she embarked on her current course of studies, she had spent two years studying psychiatric nursing in Trinity College Dublin, and, without any hesitation or any prompting on my part, began a searingly honest account of her own battles: 'I actually suffered with my own mental health problems. I struggled with an eating disorder and self-harm, all throughout my teenage years. I had to take a step back from psychiatric nursing and look after myself, rather than others. I just wasn't in the right frame of mind at the time. I took time away from my studies to let myself get better. I always wanted a career where I could help other people; I loved the nursing while I was there but I found it very difficult to balance it with all the sport I was playing.'

She then detailed how the particular eating disorder she struggled with affected her: 'It was bulimia nervosa but I also had anorexic tendencies. I went through periods when I would I have been skinny enough but then periods of binge eating and purging. It probably would have started at age 12 or 13 when I started secondary school, but it probably didn't become a big problem until I was 16 or 17, my late teens basically. It took a while for me to talk about it. I had a couple of very rough years. I was stuck in a cycle of self-harm: I didn't want to get out of it but I couldn't get out of it either.'

Throughout this period she was playing under-age inter-county football for Dublin, and although the bulimia affected her football 'in terms of moods and energy levels', sport for Tyrrell was her only escape: 'It was the only thing that gave me a bit of relief from the constant battle that was going on in my head. It was nice to be able to get away from my thoughts for a couple of hours and be with friends and to enjoy something I loved. Because of my eating disorder and the self-harm, I didn't want to communicate with anybody. It has a tendency to make you withdraw from people, but the sport didn't allow me to. That social bond with the girls was something that kept me coming back to training and kept me sane at the time. Even though I didn't realise what a big impact they were having on keeping me going, it was fantastic to have the girls there. None of them really knew the struggles I was going through, but when it all started to come out that I was struggling with these problems, they were so supportive.'

Tyrrell gives a fascinating insight into starting to look at how her illness was affecting the one thing that was keeping her going: 'At those times when I would have struggled with my performance … I often thought,

"Imagine how good I could be if I didn't have an eating disorder, imagine how if I really put 100% into it!'" It seems that some of the perfectionistic tendencies that she admits 'leave you vulnerable' were also helping her back towards good health. It is with a wisdom beyond her years that she explains: 'Sometimes people say that must have been tough growing up for you, but I don't think I would change it because it has made me the person I am today. I have a different outlook on life now; I know what I have been through and what I have come through. It has made me the person I am and for that reason I wouldn't change anything.'

It is somewhat ironic that rugby became the sport of choice for someone who has struggled with issues around food, eating, body image and weight, when one considers that both male and female players are required to bulk up, and this is certainly not lost on Tyrrell: 'At the beginning of the sevens programme, when nutrition became a huge thing, I was thinking, "Oh, it is very easy to slip back into the patterns of an eating disorder", but I just have to keep focused on how I have to be healthy to keep performing to my best, to be putting in that fuel for the body. It is all about positivity and talking about those negative thoughts. I am very open about what I have gone through and I am not afraid to tell somebody that "Look, I have been having these thoughts. I just have to stay positive."' What makes the irony even more poignant is that she has been marked out as a player who is required to gain weight in muscle: 'Actually, in the sevens programme, I am what is known as a "maximiser", so I have been given a target weight and I have to try to reach that. It is quite hard because people think you can eat what you like, but you have to be putting on the right kind of weight. You can't be eating takeaways every night! You have to be doing it the healthy way because they want you to gain muscle. When I first came into the programme and I was told there would be daily weigh-ins, I thought, "Oh, this is very daunting and how will I cope with this?" I had my reservations and now I have embraced it as a challenge and I am now thinking, "Okay, I am going to put on weight because it will make me a better player, and if this is something that will make me a better rugby player, it is something I want to do."'

Tyrrell seems to find the environment of the Ireland sevens programme refreshing and supportive because, as part of their daily routine, the players openly discuss issues relating to their weight due to the part nutrition plays in their training. With genuine enthusiasm she expounds on how, 'With the issue of weight, when someone reaches their target weight, there is applause all around. People would be very open talking about their weight, their target weight or their body fat percentage, where we have targets around that as well. As we have to eat very healthily we sometimes get bored of eating the same foods all the time, so we have a nutrition group and we are constantly talking about what snacks taste good but are still healthy. People are open about it because it is another part of performance and improving our performance.'

Tyrrell believes that the mental toughness she has developed as a result of all she has been through now helps her on the rugby pitch: 'I actually think I thrive on the bigger games. Other people would be getting very nervous – granted I was very nervous for my first cap against Italy. But I think I do like the pressure sometimes. I think I do make good decisions under pressure. Maybe it did help.'

The build-up to that first cap was something of a whirlwind. Trials for the fifteens squad were in December, and Ireland's Six Nations campaign began on Friday, 6 February. The players only found out the previous Sunday who would be part of the travelling squad, and departed for Florence on the Wednesday. Despite having already been capped at sevens, there was a sense of the unknown for Tyrrell heading into that trip. The excitement can still be heard in her voice a few months later as she says: 'It was my first experience of flying with a fifteens team. I didn't really know what the atmosphere would be like. I had never travelled in such a large group because in sevens, there is always so few of us. We are taking up the whole plane here!' Naturally, there were also doubts: 'I would have put myself under a lot of pressure, wondering if I could do enough. I had a lot to live up to. There was a lot of other girls back home who would have loved to have been in the position I was in. I had to keep telling myself that I was going to work as hard as I could and keep doing the best as I could and hopefully that could be enough.' She continues, giving a behind-the-scenes glimpse of the match-day build-up: 'I felt Friday, the day of the game, was a very long day because we were up so early. You have a few meetings in the morning but you have the rest of the day off. I just thought that six o'clock or whatever time it was for us to leave, that we were never going to get there. I was very nervous. I decided to chat to friends and family from home; it really helped me calm my nerves because I had a lot of doubts, like "Am I good enough?" or "If I don't play well, I won't get picked again ..." It was the moment I had to prove myself.'

Tyrrell pays tribute to some of the more senior players who welcomed her and fellow uncapped players Sarah Mimnagh, Fiona O'Brien, Katie Norris, Katie Fitzhenry and Sene Naoupu on that first away trip. Veteran scrum half Tania Rosser receives a special mention for 'acting like a mammy to lots of us new caps and younger girls. Tania has such a wealth of experience; she has been through it all. Nearly any situation I may have worried about, she would say something like, "Yeah, I remember when that happened to me." It was fantastic to chat to her because it would calm your nerves. She would look after you and make sure you were eating enough or that we weren't late for meetings.' It seems that this maternal role comes naturally to New Zealand-born Rosser, the only member of the current Ireland women's squad who is a mother. She famously returned to the rugby field just three months after the birth of her son Serge (named in honour of the legendary French full-back Serge Blanco), and was playing touch rugby until she was six months pregnant. Young Serge, now seven, was a common sight in celebratory post-match photos with his mother during last year's World Cup in France. Tyrrell recalls with great fondness how Rosser, along with fellow Irish-Kiwi Naoupu (who came to Ireland when her back-row husband George joined Connacht), 'set up a little hairdressing salon on the day of games, so we could all get our hair done': having tightly and neatly plaited hair is a must for any long-haired female rugby player due to the game's contact.

The warmth and intimacy of the players' pre-match rituals is a world away from the bruising encounters they face on the field of play. That night in Florence, it certainly was not a case of playing under the Tuscan sun at the Stadio Mario Lodigiani, where the conditions were bitter and blustery: or, as Tyrrell bluntly put it, 'It was a horrible night; the weather was crap'. Gavin Cummiskey of the *Irish Times* and myself were the only two Irish members of the media present. I was in a rather frantic state as I was filing match reports as a freelancer for five different media outlets including the *Irish Independent, Irish Examiner* and *Irish Daily Star*. The small community stadium seemed a world away from the grandeur of Rome's Stadio Olimpico where we would cover the men the next day. Although we sat shivering with our laptops perched precariously on a garden table – a makeshift media workspace – it was a privilege to be there that evening, helping to chronicle the beginning of Ireland's women's 2015 Six Nations journey. Also, our hosts from local club Firenze Rugby 1931 were particularly welcoming, providing pairs of gloves and delicious local gourmet sausages to compensate for the chilly conditions. The match was far from vintage, but it is always interesting to watch a team under a new regime. Of the six new names on the team sheet, Tyrrell started the match while the other five were on the bench.

After a lively opening quarter and a period of persistent pressure from the Girls in Green, newly appointed captain Briggs opened the scoring, with a try off the back of the scrum. The full-back converted her own try.

The remainder of the first half was played at a frantic pace as the Italians applied great pressure, and full-back Manuela Furlan created half a chance with some rapier-like runs. However, the Irish showed their grit and determination. English referee Sarah Cox awarded a string of penalties to Ireland due to persistent infringements around the ruck from Italy. The stiff breeze prevented Briggs from taking Ireland's score to double digits before half-time.

After the interval, the Italian resistance gave in with just four minutes on the clock when blindside flanker Paula Fitzpatrick powered over the line. Briggs failed to add the extras, but atoned for this miss minutes later with a superb long-range penalty kick. At 58 minutes the Italian defence wilted as outside centre Jenny Murphy scored from her own grubber kick. Briggs' conversion attempt drifted wide. Despite her patchy placekicking, Briggs led by example and it looked as if she had scored a brace at 63 minutes, only for the try to be disallowed. Two minutes later number eight Heather O'Brien crossed the line; Briggs' conversion took the score to 25-nil. Fitzpatrick sealed a brace for herself with just five minutes left to play. The final play of the match resulted in a consolation score from Azzurre replacement Maria Magatti. I wrote in my notebook that evening: 'The 30 points to 5 victory is not just a positive start to the Six Nations but also shows indications of a bright dawn to a new era in Irish Women's rugby after the departure of significant figures such as former head coach Philip Doyle and long time captain Fiona Coghlan.'

Further observations I jotted down that night included: 'Newly appointed head coach Tom Tierney would be impressed with his charges' composure, captain Niamh Briggs leading from example with a woman of the match performance and a lively debut from Hannah Tyrrell on the wing.' I can distinctly remember Tyrrell dashing colt-like down her wing, showing great endeavour. However, her own version of events is much more insightful, coming from the heart of the action: 'It was not a night for wingers. I was very disappointed not to be getting much ball but some people would say that is not a bad thing because if you get [only] a bit of ball you are allowed to grow into the game gradually, but I just wanted the ball. I just wanted to do my job properly. I just wanted to get out there. Once I had gotten out on to the pitch, I was absolutely fine.'

When I interviewed players for this book, when asked about how they played in a particular match they customarily tended to point out their errors rather than what they did right, showing their hunger and desire to improve. According to Tyrrell, 'I dropped the ball a couple of times under the high kicks and stuff. I was a little nervous but I had some good moments and I settled myself a bit. Getting out to sing the anthem was probably one of the proudest moments for me. My whole family were in Kiely's pub with all the Belvo girls watching. I knew they were all watching.' Even so, Tyrrell again showed her tendency to be frank: 'As … nice as it was to be on the pitch for my first cap, it was nice to get it out of the way as well.'

A tradition Ireland's women share with their male counterparts is that players after making their debut must stand up and sing a solo, regardless of musical ability. Tyrrell chose 'Cups', from the hit film *Pitch Perfect* – and, according to prop Ailis Egan, she acquitted herself well! This was an apt choice when you consider the 'girl-power' premise of the movie, featuring the struggles of an all-girl college singing group. In particular, one verse pertains to the beginning of a journey and mentions 'sights to give you shivers' along the way.

The journey for Hannah Tyrrell and for Ireland's women had significant stops to come in Ashbourne, Swansea and Cumbernauld – and there would be 'sights to give you shivers'.

ITALY 5, IRELAND 30
STADIO MARIO LODIGIANI, 6 FEBRUARY 2015

Italy: M Furlan; M Veronese (B Rigoni 53), S Stefan (M Magatti 68), M Cioffi (P Zangirolmami 53), M Sillari; V Schiavon, S Barattin; E Cucchiella, L Cammarano, M Bettoni; F Severin, A Trevisan; I Arrighetti (V Ruzza 49), E Giordano, S Gaudino (capt).

Ireland: N Briggs; H Tyrrell, J Murphy, J Shiels (K Fitzhenry 69), A Miller (S Naoupu 75); N Stapleton, L Muldoon (T Rosser 78); R O'Reilly (F Hayes 69), G Bourke (S Mimnagh 75), A Egan (F O'Brien 75); S Spence, ML Reilly (O Fitzsimons 69); P Fitzpatrick (K Norris 75), C Molloy, H O'Brien.

Referee: S Cox (England).

Scoring sequence: 20 mins: Briggs try, con 0–7; 44 mins: Fitzpatrick try 0–12; 56 mins: Briggs pen 0–15; 58 mins: Murphy try 0–20; 65 mins: O'Brien try 0–25; 74 mins: Fitzpatrick try 0–30; 80 mins: Magatti try 5–30.

6

ITALY: MIKE ROSS

Peter O'Reilly

For a tournament that prides itself on its warlike qualities, the Six Nations launches itself with a flurry of politeness. That flurry occurs annually in the exclusively genteel surrounds of the Hurlingham Club on the banks of the Thames, near Fulham – all neoclassical porticos and croquet lawns. One day in January, the club is invaded by flocks of media folk, all desperate for words of aggressive intent from six coaches and six captains, none of whom are willing to oblige, and all of whom are there mainly to fulfil contractual obligations. They'll tell you that the Six Nations is all about momentum. They'll tell you that nobody fancies opening the campaign in Edinburgh, or London, or Paris, or Rome, or Cardiff, or indeed Dublin.

In other words, they're looking to avoid saying anything that might provide motivational fuel for their opponents.

As coach to the reigning champions, Joe Schmidt was extra cautious in his utterances, ultra-diplomatic. Yes, of all the European teams, Ireland were highest in the World Rugby rankings at third and yes, that made them the bookies' favourites, not least because England, the second favourites, were scheduled to play in Dublin. But Schmidt saw no value to his players in being tournament favourites – or favouritism, as he called it – and therefore he saw no value in that fact at all.

'Favouritism is a superficial thing,' he said. 'There's nothing tangible. You can't reach out and say: "Well, we can take that favouritism and do something useful with it." I think we try to remain as pragmatic as we can be and just say right, what can we do that actually affects our preparation in a tangible way, that can help improve an individual in his skill execution or preparation or our continuity, our clarity, our unity in what we're trying to do? It's not something that is mentioned in camp.'

His skipper echoed Schmidt's sentiments. 'It's just important not to get distracted with rankings,' said Paul O'Connell. 'I don't think once since Joe's taken over have we really looked at the bigger picture. I am sure they do – the coaching staff and the management, in the background. But we had a week-long camp over Christmas and all we did was prepare for Italy – our attack, our defence, set-piece for Italy. It's just a simple way of avoiding any distractions.'

You could understand Schmidt's caution, for the stakes were even higher than normal. Ireland were aiming to achieve what they hadn't achieved since 1949, and win a second consecutive championship title. They were due to start their defence against two teams – Italy and France – who just happened to be pool opponents in the World Cup later in the year, so there were psychological points to be scored as well as real ones. But from a few weeks out Schmidt knew that he wouldn't be able to select his chief play-maker for Rome, as Johnny Sexton was fulfilling a mandatory 12-week rest from contact after suffering his fourth consecutive concussion in a cal-endar year, towards the end of the Australia game, when he clashed heads with Rob Kearney. With Paddy Jackson also out injured for the duration of the tournament, it was boiling down to a contest between the two Ians, Keatley and Madigan – neither of them a seasoned Test player – to see who would start at 10 in the Stadio Olimpico. On top of that, there were doubts over the fitness of Conor Murray after he hurt his neck playing in Zebre on the second weekend in January and would miss Munster's final two pool games in the European Champions Cup. Ireland might be able to handle the absence of one world-class half-back, but two?

Schmidt's problems didn't stop there. Cian Healy and Sean O'Brien, two players recovering from long-term injury, looked unlikely to be back in time for Rome, and there was uncertainty over the centre combination – remember, this was also Ireland's first Six Nations in 15 years *sans* Brian O'Driscoll. Finally, there was a rather inconvenient situation at tight-head prop, with Leinster coach Matt O'Connor suddenly refusing to pick the incumbent, Mike Ross.

This was more than just inconvenient for Michael Avery Ross. He'd turned 35 just before Christmas and the perception of his being on the last lap of a late-developing career was reinforced when the IRFU offered him only a one-year extension to his contract when he'd been hoping for at least two more years. If he didn't start for Ireland, he knew he wouldn't be on the bench – he's not the sort of player who accelerates the pace of a game or adds impact. And if he wasn't in the match-day squad, it was a short hop to obsolescence. The way that he dealt with this appalling vista says much about his resilience.

Ross's survival instincts are pretty well honed at this stage. The first time he knew he had a problem was sitting at home in Rathgar the second Saturday in January, watching Leinster play Cardiff Blues on the TV – O'Connor had told him to rest for the weekend to get ready for the Champions Cup game against Castres at the RDS the following Saturday. His two young understudies, Marty Moore and Tadhg Furlong, both had good outings, with Furlong scoring a try.

'I knew immediately that this mightn't be good news,' says Ross. 'What we needed was not just to beat Castres but to score tries – and I've scored one try in my entire professional career! At UCD on the Monday, they announce the training teams and I'm not in the first one or the second one – that's when you know. I've been around long enough. Suddenly your mind is racing – if I don't make the Castres game, I won't make Wasps; if I don't make Wasps, I won't make Rome; if I don't make Rome, I'm goosed for the Six Nations.'

He approached O'Connor, who confirmed his fears. The lads had gone well in Cardiff. Leinster's scrum had been struggling a little, and that was Ross's main area of responsibility. They'd be giving the lads a go. He had to take it on the chin.

'You realise you're not going to change his mind there and then so there's no point arguing it,' he says. 'You're pretty pissed off, obviously. Everybody likes to be valued, to think that their contribution is something that's needed and sport is no different. But you go away and look at it and see if he [O'Connor] has a point. If he does, what can I do about it? Greg Feek [Ireland's scrum coach] was handy to have, as an extra pair of eyes. So was Enda [McNulty, the performance coach], who gets you to focus on your strengths – scrummaging, mauling, cleaning out. You dominate in training as much as possible. I also talked to Marco [Caputo, Leinster's scrum coach]. I come from a scientific background, so data is king – the more viewpoints you can get, the better.

'At the same time, the most important viewpoint is your own. You know the score, you know what you need to do. You've done it before you can do it again. The other thing you need to do is to help prepare the lads to play. The week of the Castres game, I played the role of Ramiro Herrera, their tight-head. What does he like to do in the scrum? He likes to come in hard at the hooker, so I tried to replicate that. We've all seen the lads who have been dropped and they have thrown their toys out of the pram, going around the place with a big sulky head on them. I didn't want to be that guy. Maybe I was sulking but I didn't want to show it.'

Watching Leinster put 50 points on Castres wasn't as pleasant as it might have been – both Moore and Furlong scored tries. He knew he was unlikely to make the final pool game away to Wasps, which left just one possible outing before the Italy game – for the Wolfhounds, against the England Saxons in Cork on Friday 30 January, eight days before Rome. A phone call from Schmidt before the Castres game had provided a glimmer of hope.

'Joe told me he could give me no guarantees but that there would be an opportunity somewhere along the line,' says Ross. 'We have known each other a while now. He knows how I operate. He'd show a degree of loyalty but if I didn't perform that's where it would end. I knew I would probably get an opportunity against the Saxons. That would be my sink or swim moment.'

Ross stayed afloat. Having gone almost a month without any game-time put a strain on his aerobic capacity but he lasted 50 minutes and Ireland's scrum was steady. He still had a nervous wait until Tuesday morning, when Schmidt would read out the team, but having been included in the lineouts rehearsal on the Monday was a positive sign. He knew for definite the following morning.

'What Mike gives us is solidity in the scrum,' said Schmidt at the team announcement. 'I know he was well underdone before the autumn and I thought he hung in really well against what is a very strong South African pack, while Australia are also very tricky to play in the front row. Mike has delivered in the past and we're hopeful he'll deliver again.'

And Ross's reaction? 'I was pretty happy, obviously,' he says. 'It's tough on Marty but that fellow has another 10–15 years of top-class ahead of him. He's a good lad; we have a good relationship. The three of us tight-heads do, actually. You'd think we'd be at each other's throats but no. We'd often be reviewing games together, talking through our roles for different plays. Plus, I suppose we have a few things in common, like the love of food!'

As it turned out, Ross's salvation was way down the list of talking points from the team announcement. Tight-head props don't get the same attention as out-halves, and there was news at out-half – Ian Keatley had got the nod ahead of Ian Madigan, who'd struggled to make a positive impression in Cork, when he was operating largely on the back foot. Keatley had the advantage of playing regularly with Conor Murray, who'd been passed fit to play. If this was a bonus for Schmidt, so too was the inclusion of Sean O'Brien, who hadn't played a Test match since the New Zealand game 14 months previously, but who'd looked his old self against the Saxons. His experience would come in handy, especially in the absence of Sexton and also of Jamie Heaslip, whose shoulder niggle meant he was set to miss his first Six Nations game in all of seven years. Jordi Murphy had been given the nod at number eight. In midfield, Schmidt had gone for Robbie Henshaw and Jared Payne, who had looked good against the Boks but were still getting to know each other. All told, there were eight changes from the team that had clinched the title in Paris 10 months before – great for building squad depth, if a little nerve-racking for the coach, who described himself as 'paranoid' beforehand. 'I often deal in worst-case scenarios,' he said, only half-jokingly.

For Ross, Rome is a place with happy associations. He'd made his first Six Nations start here, four years previously, when a late Ronan O'Gara drop-goal had spared Ireland's blushes, and, of course, he loved the Eternal City. International rugby teams stay in some swish hotels but for Ross, the Westin Excelsior on the Via Veneto is the swishest. It's only a short stroll from the gardens of the Villa Borghese, a sublime, sunlit backdrop for lineout drills on the morning of the game.

The setting may have been beautiful to behold but in truth, the game was not, with Ireland taking a low-risk, high-work-rate approach to grinding out their 26–3 victory. They led just 9–3 at the break after a nervous start, having been thrown by the sight of O'Brien tweaking a hamstring at the end of the warm-up – only minutes before kick-off, Tommy O'Donnell learnt that he'd be starting at seven. Paul O'Connell fluffed his kick-off reception, while Keatley kicked poorly from the hand to begin with – though the out-half would soon settle down, landing all five of his shots at goal. Reassurance came from the solidity of the scrum, as Ross thoroughly vindicated his selection.

Watching the DVD a few days later, it was noticeable how much stick he had to take from team-mates when Ireland were in defence – on the referee's microphone, Rob Kearney can be heard berating him for wandering out of position: 'For fuck's sake, Rossy, push up!', and so forth. The target of all this anger is well used to such 'encouragement'.

'Taking shit from full-backs is part and parcel of the gig,' says Ross. 'Stick Rob in the scrum for 20 seconds, and see how quickly his legs move after that! But they're not roaring at me to make themselves feel good. It's just about making sure the system works. I was happy with the way the game went, especially the scrums. Playing Italy on their patch, and especially in the first game of the Six Nations, when they're at full strength, it's more about making sure that they don't get any oxygen from their scrum. It's very important to them. If they're driving over you or taking your ball or winning penalties, you can see their chests swell up, or they start patting you on the head and slapping each other on the back. But if they're pushing and shoving for 12 seconds and going nowhere, they can deflate a little bit. They've gotten into us a couple of times before over there, so we were happy.

'You're not going to put 60 points on them in the first game, not over there. If you want to put a score on Italy, it generally doesn't happen until the end of the tournament, when they're tired and they've picked up a few injuries – just look at the trends over the last two Six Nations. First up, it's about keeping the scoreboard ticking over, denying them access. Keep squeezing them and the scores will eventually come. They might still be there at 60 minutes but if you keep that pressure on, eventually you will get a reward for it.'

Which is exactly how things worked out. The critical moment came in the 64th minute when Italy's hooker, Leonardo Ghiraldini, was sent to the sin-bin for collapsing the Ireland maul 10 metres from his own try-line, with disastrous consequences for his team. Ireland's lead was just 12–3 at this point but that rapidly became 19–3 as Murray burrowed over near the ruck after Murphy and Sean Cronin had carried forcibly off the lineout.

After such a long wait, one try brought another – like the 46A bus, as someone mentioned. The only Italian player to touch the ball between tries was Kelly Haimona, and that was when he banged the restart downfield. Ireland carried the ball back with intent before the newly arrived Madigan sent O'Donnell up the middle on a rampaging 40-metre run through Andrea Masi's horribly weak attempted tackle and under the posts for the score that made victory absolutely secure.

Ireland had been ordinary enough by their standards, offering precious little by way of creativity, yet here they were, 23 points clear. You wondered what the Italian supporters made of it. After a rousing rendition of 'Fratelli d'Italia' before kick-off, we were well into the final quarter before they raised another sustained cheer, when Luke McLean broke down the left flank. Why do they continue to turn up in their thousands to this fabulous stadium when they get so little joy in return? Since they had beaten Ireland in 2013, Italy had won only two matches – against Fiji and Japan. 'With Italian rugby fans, it's not about the result,' explained Paolo, an Italian colleague. 'It's the same when we go to the opera. We know what will happen at the end. It's the quality of the performance that we have come to see.'

Well, it was a disappointing performance; high on effort, woefully short on imagination – how depressing to see the great Sergio Parisse reduced to the role of battering ram. To their credit, Italy did keep battering until the end, only to see Haimona denied a late try by the Television Match Official, who spotted the hint of a knock-on by Parisse. 'I remember thinking that this could be really important by the end of the tournament,' says Ross. 'I was watching from the stand at this stage, having done my shift, thinking: 'Don't let them in, lads, don't let them in. While we weren't beating them by a lot of points, another team could, so it was very important to make sure that our points difference was as good as it could be. Obviously the main aim is to win a Grand Slam but that's a damn hard thing to do. We knew from last year that every point counts.'

Most observers were just content that another ugly game in the Italian capital was over. 'None of the pictures from Rome are worth keeping,' wrote Denis Walsh in the *Sunday Times*. 'As a spectacle, it was draining. All of the style was in the outcome.' In the *Irish Times*, Gerry Thornley proposed that 'you can never forget a weekend in Rome, but you can certainly forget Irish wins there'.

As for Schmidt, he conceded that his team had been '20–30 per cent' off where they needed to be, certainly in comparison with England, who had ignited the tournament with a storming comeback in Cardiff the previous night, eventually winning 21–16. But this had been a good test of squad depth and players like Keatley, Murphy and O'Donnell had grown into the game. At the same time, Schmidt was relieved to know that he'd be able to call upon leaders like Sexton, Heaslip and

O'Brien the following weekend against France.

'We had a scratchy start but I'm really happy with the way we got past that and then really squeezed Italy out of the game,' Schmidt said. 'We got asked to defend at times and we put our hands up and defended really strongly. When we did attack it wasn't as fluent as it might have been – I think we were anxious, we were snatching at things. But after that first 20 minutes, I'm really happy with the next 50 minutes that we put together.

'It was a massive banana skin so I'm relieved that we got through, that we have a points differential that we can be happy with. We know that there's going to be incredibly tough battles in the next two games and beyond. There's nothing easy in this tournament.'

And Mike Ross? He allowed himself a glass of Chianti at the post-match function back in town. 'I felt satisfied to have come through the game and to have done pretty well. I was thinking: This is something I can build on. I didn't want to let Joe down. He had given me an opportunity and that's a huge thing. He could have said: "Grand, you're done and dusted. Thanks for the memories." But he gave me an opportunity.

'Joe was happy afterwards but of course, a couple of days later, when he'd analysed the game on tape, he told me my ruck accuracy hadn't been good enough and I needed to work on it [laughs]. It's not like he'd ever let you get comfortable!'

ITALY 3, IRELAND 26

STADIO OLIMPICO, 7 MARCH 2015

Italy: A Masi (G Venditti 77); L Sarto, M Campagnaro (T Allan 64), L Morisi, L McLean; K Haimona, E Gori; M Aguero (A De Marchi 53), L Ghiraldini (F Minto 75), M Castrogiovanni (D Chistolini 69); J Furno, G Biagi (M Barbini 75); A Zanni (M Barbini 47) (M Fuser for Barbini, 68), F Minto (A Manici 69), S Parisse (capt).
Sinbinned: Ghiraldini (64–74 mins).

Ireland: R Kearney; T Bowe, J Payne (F Jones 68), R Henshaw, S Zebo; I Keatley (I Madigan 66), C Murray (I Boss 69); J McGrath (J Cronin 68), R Best (S Cronin, 47), M Ross (M Moore 52); D Toner, P O'Connell (capt); P O'Mahony (I Henderson 66), T O'Donnell, J Murphy.

Referee: P Gauzère (France).

Scoring sequence: 7 mins: Keatley pen 0–3; 21 mins: Keatley pen 0–6; 37 mins: Keatley pen 0–9; 40+1 mins: Haimona pen 3–9; 58 mins: Keatley pen 3–12; 65 mins: Murray try, Keatley con 3–19; 67 mins: O'Donnell try, Madigan con 3–26.

7

FRANCE: TOM TIERNEY

Kate Rowan

'Famous yet infamous' is how many would regard the events of 12 June 1999 in Brisbane's Lang Park from an Irish rugby perspective. The fame comes from the fact that some 20-year-old called Brian, yet to have even played for his province, pulled on a baggy cotton jersey bearing the number 13 to make his Test debut. That night was perhaps the beginning of a new era for Irish rugby as it marked the introduction to the world stage of a player who would prove to be one of the most talented of his generation, and would go on to become the face of his sport in Ireland. The infamy comes from the fact that Australia racked up a 46 points to 10 scoreline: the Wallabies' biggest ever winning margin over Ireland.

Almost 15 years later, in the week leading up to Brian O'Driscoll's last international appearance in March 2014, as Ireland's men were on the cusp of snatching the Six Nations title in the Stade de France, *ESPN Scrum* ran a feature about that Brisbane Test. Its author, Tom Hamilton, has a wonderful knack for telling the stories behind the headlines. The article looked at two players who made their Ireland debuts alongside O'Driscoll, asking 'Where are they now?' of wing Matt Mostyn and scrum-half Tom Tierney.

Within a year of publication of that piece, Tierney was making another debut for Ireland, this time as head coach of Ireland's women. When asked to compare how he feels now compared with then, his response is philosophical: 'It's two different things and two different people. I was such a young guy when it all happened that it was all a bit of a blur.' With a chuckle he indicates his salt-and-pepper hair: 'Now, I'm older, wiser, greyer and it's totally different now. I appreciate it more with age. As a younger guy it is a brilliant memory to have but it does feel different … it is 16 years since I made my international debut, so it is a long time. I've changed. I'm 38 now, and I was just turning 23 then. It is just one of those things.'

In the years between earning his first Ireland cap as a 22-year-old and beginning his tenure in late 2014 with Ireland's women, Tierney had a playing career that included a further seven international appearances, including playing at the 1999 Rugby World Cup. At club level, a stint at his home province Munster was followed by a move across the Irish Sea to Leicester Tigers, which took in two seasons from 2002 to 2004, and then back to Ireland for four seasons at Connacht.

Unfortunately for Tierney, his retirement was enforced due to shoulder and ankle injuries. From the change in his tone of voice from describing his earlier career to the later part, it would seem that he endured a difficult period: 'It was hard because you are a rugby player all your life. That last year in Connacht I never played, just trying to get back. At the end of it, then, it was just about cutting my losses.' It was during that period of being injured at the tail-end of his career that Tierney discovered his passion for coaching: 'While at Connacht I helped out with Galwegians as the backs coach for their senior team – it was just to keep me going because of the injury and I found out I enjoyed it. When I was going to retire it was a question of was I going to move totally out of rugby or stay in rugby. I decided to stay in rugby and give coaching a fair crack of the whip ... seven years now and I haven't looked back.'

Tierney's approach to growing his coaching CV was to 'start at the very bottom, as coaching and playing are two totally different things.' So he worked his way up, starting at Tipperary Town's Clanwilliam RFC, close to where he had settled with his wife, Mary. At this time he also coached in his native Limerick City, working with Crescent Comprehensive School. He then gained All Ireland League (AIL) experience coaching with Garryowen, with whom he had played, and then on to Cork Constitution, while building further exposure to under-age coaching at Glenstal Abbey School. He was proving himself to be one of the brightest emerging home-grown coaches.

When women's fifteens became part of the IRFU's high-performance unit, Tierney was called 'out of the blue' and asked if he would take on the role of Ireland women's coach to work alongside director of women's and sevens rugby, Australian Anthony Eddy. This was initially on an interim basis, but he has since secured a permanent position. It was his first time coaching women, and his attitude comes across as pragmatic and forward-thinking: 'You hear all sorts of things about the differences between men and women, but at the end of the day the girls are rugby players and that is how we run it. You just have to do your job as a coach; whether it is a men's team, a women's team or a schoolboy team, the key principles are the same: you are honest, you know exactly what you are talking about and you are organised. You go from there and hopefully you build an environment that is a winning environment.' When questioned on the origins of this 'women as rugby players, nothing more, nothing less' attitude, he does not hesitate: 'I am surrounded by women at home; I have my wife and two little girls. Isabel is five and Julia has just turned one. Whether I like it or not, I am well able to deal with women!' Getting back to serious business, he concludes: 'As long as you are going into the job in the right frame of mind, and dealing with it and having yourself correct, it doesn't matter who you are dealing with.'

There is one intriguing aspect of Tierney's sporting journey that would strike a chord with many of the women he now coaches. He was a relative latecomer to playing 'serious' rugby, as he had enjoyed some success at his first love, soccer. He recalls: 'My dream goal as a young guy was to play for the Republic of Ireland in soccer. That dream was dashed at 16 or 17 when I knew I wasn't good enough. I grew up supporting Fairview Rangers, a famous junior soccer club in Limerick. I played in the famous Kennedy Cup and captained Limerick in that.' He goes on to tell just how close he came to a professional football career as a young centre-half: 'I was then offered trials in Ipswich, Nottingham Forest, Sheffield Wednesday and Peterborough. I went over to all those places and tried out. It was a very, very competitive environment for a young 14 or 15 year old. It wasn't for me at the time: I came home ... and decided not to focus on soccer, slowly but surely moved into playing rugby.' When asked about sporting heroes who inspired him during his formative years, Tierney doesn't hesitate: 'Without a shadow of a doubt: Paul McGrath. Paul McGrath was my one and only hero. Not necessarily off the field but on the field. He was the guy [on whom] I tried to model and replicate my play.'

The soccer nostalgia starts to fade as he again shows a pragmatic nature: 'That is how short it was [my soccer career], but soccer was always something I loved and I was quite good at it but I had to have a shift in the mindset at the time. When I did make the transition from soccer to rugby, it was starting to move into the professional game ... that is why I decided to move into that and take rugby seriously. Once I focused totally on rugby, building my way up through the under-age set-up in Munster and Ireland, then my goal changed to playing rugby for Ireland.'

When Tierney speaks about having to 'learn' rugby at a slightly older age

Above: Fiona Coghlan and Philip 'Goose' Doyle on *The Late Late Show* in 2013. Their appearance shows the increased media interest in Ireland's women's rugby.

Right: Tania Rosser celebrates with her son Serge after Ireland beat her birth nation of New Zealand in the 2014 Women's Rugby World Cup.

Left and below left:
Rob Kearney – from the joy of scoring against New Zealand to go 19–0 up in the Aviva Stadium in November 2013 and a possible first-ever win for Ireland over the All Blacks ... to the despair of a narrow last-minute defeat.

Below: The end of the age of BOD. Brian O'Driscoll in the Stade de France dressing rooms after Ireland clinched the 2014 Six Nations title.

Above: Joe Schmidt chats with former Ireland women's coach Philip 'Goose' Doyle during the 2014 Women's Rugby World Cup in France.

Below: Nora Stapleton with her grandmother Iris in Donegal county colours in Croke Park for the 2014 All Ireland Gaelic Football Final.

Above: Paul O'Connell and Niamh Briggs share a light-hearted moment at the Six Nations media launch at the Hurlingham Club, London.

Right: Hannah Tyrrell in Dublin Airport before Ireland's women set off for Florence and their first match of the 2015 Six Nations Championship.

Above: Joe Schmidt and tight-head prop Mike Ross, who went into the 2015 Six Nations with much to prove, at Ireland's Carton House training base.

Right: In the absence of Jonathan Sexton, Munster's Ian Keatley started at 10 for Ireland against Italy in the Stadio Olimpico.

Above: Tommy O'Donnell was promoted to starting openside against Italy when Sean O'Brien was injured; he went on to score in the match.

Below: Marie Louise 'Maz' Reilly wins a lineout for Ireland against Italy on a wet and windy evening in the Stadio Mario Lodigiani, Florence.

Right: Tom Tierney on his Ireland debut in Brisbane versus Australia in 1999 (some centre called Brian also made his Test bow that evening).

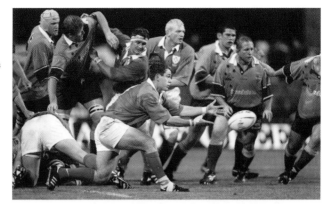

Right: Sixteen years later, as head coach of Ireland's women's team, Tierney looks on as his side face France in Ashbourne.

Below: Ireland's outside centre Jenny Murphy is consoled by teammate Marie Louise Reilly after Ireland lose 5–10 to France in Ashbourne.

Left: Back in Carton House, Paul O'Connell trains as Jonathan Sexton and Rob Kearney look on two days before taking on France.

Below: After much talk in the build-up of how France's Mathieu Bastareaud would target Jonathan Sexton, the two players share a post-match hug.

Above: Scrum-half Larissa Muldoon scores Ireland's only try en route to a historic win against World Champions England in Ashbourne.

Below: Conor Murray celebrates as the ball goes out of play in the Aviva Stadium as Ireland beat France 18–11.

Above: Joe Schmidt looks on as Paul O'Connell and Robbie Henshaw train in the Sportsground, Galway, leading up to Ireland's clash against England.

Below: Ireland's Robbie Henshaw scores his first try in the green of Ireland despite the efforts of England's Alex Goode.

Left: Heather O'Brien strikes a pose at Áras an Uachtaráin on International Women's Day on 8 March ahead of Ireland's fixture against Wales the following week.

Below: Paula Fitzpatrick scores Ireland's opening try against Wales in their 20–0 victory at St Helen's ground, Swansea.

Right: Jonathan Sexton tries to get the better of former British and Irish Lions colleague and Welsh outside centre Jonathan Davies.

Below: Scott Williams of Wales scores a try as his side go on to beat Ireland 23 points to 16 at the Millennium Stadium.

Above: Wing Alison Miller celebrates one of the three tries she scored against Scotland with Paula Fitzpatrick and Nora Stapleton.

Right: Captain Niamh Briggs celebrates winning the Six Nations title with her father Mike after Ireland beat Scotland.

Right: A detail from Niamh Briggs' 50th cap jersey, which she wore in Ireland's historic 73–3 win that sealed the Six Nations title for her side.

Above: Luke Fitzgerald, called in to replace Simon Zebo in Ireland's final Six Nations fixture against Scotland, pictured during the Captain's Run in Murrayfield.

Below: Rory Best with daughter Penny after Ireland beat Scotland in Murrayfield but before his side discovered that they clinched the Championship on points difference.

Above: Blindside flanker Paula Fitzpatrick
with her sister Sarah after her side sealed
Six Nations success at Broadwood Stadium.

Below: Forget *Riverdance*, it's a winners'
dance! Ireland's women celebrate winning
a second Six Nations title in three years at
Broadwood Stadium.

Above: Jamie Heaslip enjoys a moment with fans Michael Reehill and Aaron Redfern and the Six Nations trophy as the Irish team arrives home victorious to Dublin Airport.

Right: Rob Kearney and Simon Zebo take a celebratory selfie under the Murrayfield lights with the Six Nations trophy.

Right: A special moment as captains Paul O'Connell and Niamh Briggs show off their respective Six Nations trophies to the Thomond Park faithful.

than is usual, not having attended a rugby-playing school, I hear echoes of how many women describe their experience of adapting to the new sport: 'When you don't have that schools environment, you literally have to learn the game yourself and learn the technical aspects and I did that and, so, got better and better.' I ask him whether, as a 'code-hopper' like so many of Ireland's women, he can empathise with them and whether it helps him as a coach. 'I played three seasons as an amateur before turning professional. So, I can relate to where the girls are now. It is amateur sport but they train fully as professionals. I could also understand that with certain girls coming from different sports, you have to coach them differently because they are a learning a new skill set. That is something which I would hope has been a positive for the girls … I know exactly where they are coming from because I have been there myself.'

Sometimes when looking at professional or high-level amateur sport from the outside, we don't see the technical nuances that influence how players progress or who a coach may or may not select. Having covered women's rugby for the past few seasons, I found it very helpful to understand the concept of *training age*: 'It is just a realisation that some girls will have a different training age. Some would have played rugby a lot longer than other girls. It is not just about knowing who is at what level. They are all on the squad because they are all quality rugby players, but from a technical point of view, you just have to be aware who is at what level and work accordingly to get them up to speed, so we are all at the same level. Once we are all at the same level, which we like to think we are going forward, that is where the critical learning and improvements will happen.' One starts to get a sense of Tierney as a coach when he says: 'The bottom line is you have to be very honest and very upfront with the players. To get them to realise that any criticism or constructive criticism you give is not personal; it is just purely for their own well-being and benefit.'

So, what type of coach is Tierney? Is he fastidious and details-oriented like his counterpart with the men's side, Joe Schmidt? Is he a delegator like Declan Kidney? Or, going back to his footballing roots, is he one to pull out the Sir Alex Ferguson 'hairdryer' when needs be, or professorial à la Arsene Wenger? With a chuckle, he replies that 'I will probably set myself up to be shot down!' before going on: 'I try to create an environment, a very positive environment … I try to drive from myself, that it is a fun place to be. But there is a clear understanding that there is quality work to be done and there is a clear understanding that if that quality work isn't done, then there is accountability.' He carefully stresses: 'I like to think that I know exactly what I am talking about from a technical point of view. Hopefully, the players realise I am a very driven person behind the laughs and smiles; that they want to be part of the journey I try to create. I like to think I empower the players to think they are decision makers on the field and I am not a dictator. Sometimes there are opportunities given to you that you have to say, "This is how I would like it done." I like to think I can create decision makers and people who can make the hard calls for themselves on the field.' The picture Tierney paints of himself as a coach corresponds to how he is in conversation: one moment laughing heartily or making a quip, then very quickly returning to the task at hand and showing his focus and desire to succeed. A similar trait is evident in his players.

Something else that Tierney shares with his players is a habit of constantly making sure to give credit to teammates. He speaks with the same mixture of fondness, respect and admiration for the other members of the coaching staff, including Eddy, his assistant coaches Declan O'Brien and Derek 'Babs' Dowling, and head of strength and conditioning Marian Earls: 'We all want the same thing and we are all very clear about what we want, how we want to get there, how we want to get it done and how we can deliver it to the girls.' Being on the same page was imperative at the outset of this Six Nations campaign, as the new management structure had been put in place only in December.

Tierney recalls their original plan: 'It was a very short run-in, and so we planned accordingly. We knew what we had to do. It wasn't a case of us coming in cold, that we didn't know any of the girls. Obviously with the success that the girls have had over the past couple of years, we were well up to speed on what they could do, how good they were and how professional they were.' He demonstrates both humility and the 'one game at a time' approach for which players and coaches are famed: 'It was very mechanical and technical how we wanted to go about it. The credit goes to the girls; I don't think any of us would be cheeky enough to say it was down to us.'

The team got off to a winning start against Italy in Florence. 'The Italian match obviously went to plan: we won by 25 points ... We did play well but at the same time we were by far a better team. We physically outmuscled Italy that night. It was a great start but it was not a perfect start.' Tierney saw reigning Six Nations champions Les Bleues as much more formidable opposition, although Ireland had home advantage at 'Fortress Ashbourne': 'We knew the biggest test would be against France at home the following week. We only had one training session after that; just to get ourselves ready for the French.' This emphasises the amateur aspect of the women's game, notwithstanding the professional coaching team. Tierney notes that 'the last time Ireland had played them was at the Women's Rugby World Cup where France beat them. So we were under no illusions. They are very, very physical, especially up front. It was our first home game; there were a lot of nerves before the match but they were all looking forward to it at the same time.' Two changes were made to the side that had defeated the Azzurre: one was injury-enforced, as Hannah Tyrrell had suffered a concussion in training and was replaced on the wing by fellow Ireland sevens star Aoife Doyle, for what would be her first fifteens Test cap. Another member of the sevens programme, Katie Fitzhenry, was promoted from the bench to start at inside centre, with Jackie Shiels, who had been the 12 in Florence, named among the replacements.

As he experienced the pressures of playing international rugby himself, I am keen to get Tierney's perspective on the differences between being out on the field and being the one masterminding the performance behind the scenes. 'I suppose the difference is as a coach the lead-up to a match is always the most stressful, whereas when the match is on and you are watching it, you have got to be stand-offish from it; you have got to be very cold in your calculations and in your feelings. For me personally, I don't let the emotions get to me as much as some people do and I am not caught up in the game. I try to be very technical, just see the whole picture and then make strategic decisions. To make the best strategic and tactical decisions, you have to be a small bit away from the game and not get caught up in the game. Whereas as a player, the nice part is the lead-up to a game because it is all about looking forward to a big game and then the match itself is the most stressful, so everything is turned around.'

An aspect of high-level team sports that I am sure most of us who have never had access to elite dressing rooms have pondered is what coaches say to their players in the final minutes before they take the field: the team talk. Films such as *Any Given Sunday* have added to the mystique surrounding those pre-match motivational moments. In the real world, however, there seems to be a little less philosophising and tugging at heartstrings and more emphasis on keeping cool and getting the job done. Tierney explains: 'I suppose you prepare during the week. I suppose you want to give clear, concise direction but you don't want to overload the players. What I try to do is … to set the scene, there is always a technical aspect from defence and attack points of view. Then just to be aware of the opposition. It is just to break it into three parts and then you go from there. Your team talks wouldn't be longer than five or six minutes. Then that is then you pretty much finished for the day. You try to maybe say one or two things to the players in passing but you don't want to wreck their heads as they are preparing for the game themselves. I keep it as simple as possible; less is more for me, because as a player that is what I always responded to. It is something I feel the girls respond to as well.'

Yet there is a time and a place for passion and emotion. According to Anthony Eddy, Tierney can deliver a very emotive speech during jersey presentation the night before the match, pertaining to what it means to wear the green jersey for Ireland. As a foreigner, Eddy could see the positive impact of the head coach speaking about his own experiences as an international. Tierney becomes rather animated as he gives an account of this other side of motivational speaking: 'When you are talking about a green jersey, when you are talking to players who are just about to receive their jersey, it is not necessarily about cold, hard facts. You try to tap into the emotional side and what it means from an emotional point of view. I just gave them my own experiences, what it meant to me, what I felt, what I wanted to do when I had that jersey on. So, when it is tough in a game, and things are going against us, it is not like anything else; you are playing for your country, representing your country. I just try to tap into the emotional side of the brain … and hopefully get a reaction on that.' He is keen to point out that Eddy, O'Brien and Dowling also spoke at jersey presentations: 'The guys spoke brilliantly as well – it was nice to get … all the different perspectives.'

Tierney's comments on the differences between giving a pre-match team talk and speaking at the jersey presentation provide a fascinating insight into the juxtaposition of methodical planning and raw emotion, and the importance of both in the success of a team: 'If you asked me to recall a team talk, I would tell you it was about a team, what technical stuff you speak about; defence and attack. I could rap that off straight away but from an emotional side, I couldn't remember now, it just happens in the moment: you have an idea of what you want to say but you don't have a plan. You are just trying to get that genuine feeling through to the players, so they could associate with it.'

When he recalls his side's performance that chilly Friday evening in Ashbourne, there is a mixture of analysis, pride and frustration: 'The first 40 minutes, we got out of our half maybe twice … The French physically put us under severe pressure both from a forwards point of view and from a kicking point of view. Having said all that, one of the areas we really focused in on was our defence, and to have kept to nil-all at half time was absolutely amazing. It was heroic defence in that first half. Everything else? No, we actually physically stood off them when they had the ball a bit too many times.'

Much of the media coverage in the immediate aftermath concentrated on how malfunctioning floodlights cast the game into darkness just 16 seconds into the second half. A failed oil filter in the power generator was the culprit. The lights returned, only for darkness to fall once again and players to have to exit the field of play once more. After another hour, power was properly restored and play resumed at 9.15 p.m., almost two hours after kick-off.

Ireland used the extra time in the changing rooms to regroup and recover, having had to fend off wave upon wave of French attack in the first half. Tierney recalls: 'At half-time with the lights going out, I knew the French team were more upset than we were. We needed the break and it just totally transformed us. We had a good chat in the dressing rooms when the lights were still under – we drew a line under that first half.' Relatively refreshed, Ireland 'started taking it to the French. To go ahead was absolutely brilliant' – this was through a try from tight-head prop Ailis Egan off the back of terrific work from second row Marie Louise 'Maz' Reilly from a lineout maul. With a furrowed brow, Tierney continues: 'Unfortunately we threw a pass that wasn't on and they got an intercept try' scored by Caroline Boujard in the 64th minute. Full-back Jessy Tremouliere added the extras, and later slotted over a penalty to make the final scoreline Ireland 5, France 10. The coach laments that 'They won after maybe three minutes of us on their line in the last play of the game. So, there was a lot of emotion after that game, a lot of the girls were naturally disappointed that we lost.'

Did Tierney allow the pressure get to him after that first loss of his tenure? His answer is emphatic: 'You can't. If you do that you will never sleep. I got 11 years of being a professional rugby player. I have seven years now of coaching. You get used to these pressures and commitments and you have to be able to live with them. You have to deal with them. You can deal with them later on but you need your night's sleep.'

Could the players bounce back from the psychological blow of a narrow defeat? How would they react when playing England's World Champions in their next fixture? 'I think from a coaching point of view – and I stressed this to the girls after the game – the fact that the first half went the way it did and how we responded in the second half just showed how good we could be. The group were only together eight, nine weeks at the time. That was a huge positive for me. Of course you are disappointed that you have lost an international, but it was a huge step forward for us and we had to take it on the chin. We learnt the hard way. Sometimes the best way to learn is the hard way. It showed in the English match the following week that the lessons were learnt.'

IRELAND 5, FRANCE 10
MILLTOWN HOUSE, ASHBOURNE RFC,
13 FEBRUARY 2015

Ireland: N Briggs (capt); A Doyle, J Murphy, K Fitzhenry, A Miller; N Stapleton, L Muldoon (T Rosser 54); R O'Reilly (F Hayes 66), G Bourke, A Egan; S Spence, ML Reilly; P Fitzpatrick, C Molloy, H O'Brien.
Sinbinned: Fitzpatrick (73)

France: J Tremoulière; C Boujard (L Delas 80), E Poublan, C Héguy, J Billes; C Cabalou, Y Rivoalen; L Arricastre, G Mignot (capt), J Duval (Christelle Chobet 40); M André, M de Nadaï (C Ferer 68); CT Diallo, L Grand (P Rayssac 35), S N'Diaye.

Sinbinned: de Nadai (46–56 mins).

Referee: C Hodnett (England).

Scoring sequence: 47 mins: Egan try 5–0; 64 mins: Boujard try, Tremoulière con 5–7; 72 mins: Tremoulière pen 5–10.

8

FRANCE: PAUL O'CONNELL

Peter O'Reilly

For Joe Schmidt, probably the best part of his Roman weekend came back at Carton House on the Sunday evening when he sat down with Éanna Falvey, his chief medic, to learn that the physical toll of another bruising clash with the Italians was relatively light. Yes, Sean O'Brien's hamstring tightness had caused him to withdraw, but the condition of the muscle was just that – tightness – and the decision to withdraw him had been taken to avoid any risk. Yes, Rory Best had been concussed, but as he went through the rigorous testing involved in the return-to-play protocol, the initial signs were promising. Ireland rely more than most on what is known in management-speak as their 'key influencers', the players who form the spine of the team: Rob Kearney, Johnny Sexton, Conor Murray, Best, Paul O'Connell, O'Brien and Jamie Heaslip. Reassuringly for Schmidt, there was an excellent chance that this magnificent seven would all be available to face France at the Aviva the following Saturday.

'Having those people around does build a little bit of confidence,' Schmidt said. 'Hopefully it adds a bit of organisation as well. That's no disrespect to Ian Keatley, who I thought did a great job last week and he really grew into the game. But these guys have been in some tough, tight moments before, as well as some successful moments. Therefore, their decision making, their leadership, does add a bit of confidence.'

If Ireland were to win the championship, or to capture an even more treasured grand slam, the coach knew that he'd need to have his most important players around for the duration – but the way bodies were dropping elsewhere, that looked something of a long shot. You could barely open the sports pages without reading about another case of concussion. The Welsh medical team were already under fire for the fact that George North had been allowed to stay on the pitch against England in Cardiff, despite sustaining two separate concussions – and this at a time when World Rugby was under constant scrutiny for the way in which it was policing concussion management, in both the professional and amateur games. At the top end of the sport, what statistical data is available indicates clearly that the increase in player size and power coincides with an increase in the number of reported concussions, and Wales v England was an obvious case in point – as well as North,

Samson Lee and Dan Biggar were both diagnosed.

Up until the North case, the most discussed concussion case in European rugby had been Sexton's, for this broke new ground. When Sexton clashed heads with Rob Kearney towards the end of the Ireland v Australia Test the previous November, this was the player's fourth significant concussion in the space of 12 months and, in accordance with a protocol put in place by World Rugby and the Ligue Nationale de Rugby (the player was under LNR jurisdiction while employed by Racing Métro), he was forced to stand down from playing for 12 weeks. By coincidence, that 12-week mandatory 'ban' concluded on the day that France played in Dublin, but Sexton was passed fit to play by his Paris-based neurologist, Dr Jean-François Chermann.

Along with my colleague and pal, Brendan Fanning, I interviewed Sexton the week before the tournament for our weekly *Down the Blindside* podcast. He admitted to a sense of guilt at having missed so many games for Racing and was a bit uneasy that the games before and after the concussion had been for Ireland, when the club was paying his salary – his new nickname at Racing, he revealed, was Johnny Vacances (Johnny Holidays). But the laughter turned a smidgin sour the week before the France game when Bernard le Roux, a Racing team-mate who'd been selected for the Aviva, joked about Sexton: 'If I were him, I'd wear a helmet.' Philippe Saint-André, France's embattled coach, said: 'Sexton hasn't played for 12 weeks and we should really test him early on.'

What irked Sexton and the Irish management, however, was an

interview given by French journalist and ex-international Laurent Ben-ezech to the *Irish Times*, in which he criticised Sexton's selection so soon after returning to action. Benezech had caused a stir in France the previous year with the release of his book *Rugby, Ou Sont tes Valeurs?* (*Rugby, Where Are Your Values?*), which expressed serious concerns about the 'bulking up' of modern players in comparison with previous eras. Now he ruffled Irish feathers by saying: 'Ireland is in trouble as playing Sexton after what happened to him is a big mistake. I can tell you already what will be the first way France will use the ball. It will be number nine [Rory Kockott] to [Mathieu] Bastareaud, straight at Johnny Sexton.'

The IRFU issued a stern rebuke, defending the decision to select Sexton and outlining the care and rigorous testing the player had undergone to ascertain his readiness for action. For good measure, Paul O'Connell assured the media that Sexton wouldn't seek, or receive, any baby-sitting from his team-mates. 'It's the last thing he'd think or want said about him,' said O'Connell. 'Johnny is very enthusiastic about D [defence], very enthusiastic about line-speed, about knowledge of your roles in defence. He's a leader in every regard but particularly in that regard.'

While he wasn't about to express any personal concerns about rugby's safety issues in the lead-up to this, of all games, O'Connell does have some thoughts on how the number of head injuries could be reduced in the sport. As he sees it, greater incidence of concussion – and injury generally – has as much to do with poor technique as with an increase in players' power and physicality.

'It's all about line-speed now, so there are more front-on tackles than there used to be,' he told me during the Six Nations. 'I see a lot more guys – I do it myself – getting their heads on the wrong side in the tackle. Partly it's because so much of the defence practice we do is about positional defence, about getting people to fit into a system. We're really good at practising that, maybe not so good at practising tackle technique.

'One of the reasons Brian O'Driscoll was such a good tackler was his footwork. He worked on it. One of the reasons Dan Lydiate is so good at the chop-tackle is because he practises it. We tend to do less contact in training, just to be physically right from Saturday to Saturday. But technique suffers as a result.'

O'Connell also has an issue with tactical substitutions – which was topical, given the impact made by France's 145 kg replacement prop, Uini Atonio – 'a monster', according to Mike Ross – in what had otherwise been an unimpressive 15–8 victory over Scotland in Round One. As someone who tended to play the full 80 minutes, O'Connell was less than impressed by the arrival of turbo-powered bench specialists in the 50th minute, but not just for selfish reasons. He reckoned they detract from rugby's spectacle.

'Yeah, the number of subs is a big thing,' he said. 'We've now eight and sometimes six of those are forwards – guys who mightn't have the endurance for a full game but a lot of them would be big carriers, big impact players. I'm not sure what the right number is, but if you reduce it, coaches would be less inclined to use guys for impact that they need to hold back to cover injuries. That way, I think you end up with more tired guys like me dragging their asses around the pitch in the last 10 minutes. That means more space, more encouragement to play a quicker game.'

I'd been fortunate to get a private mid-tournament audience with the Ireland captain. From his early days with Munster, O'Connell had always been engaging company and a good talker. The only problem at this stage in his career was media fatigue. As someone who had captained his province, his country and the Lions, he'd been asked a lot of very similar questions and, understandably, could easily slip into autopilot mode whenever a microphone was placed before him. The trick would be to find an angle that might spark his imagination. With O'Connell's 100th cap approaching (as long as he stayed fit, he'd hit three figures in Cardiff, in Round Four), I reckoned this was an opportunity to go back in time.

I went rummaging through a box of old match programmes in search of his first game for Ireland, against Wales in 2002. I did better – a Young Munster programme from the 2000/2001 season, with a team photo of the club's Munster Junior Cup-winning team of 1999. O'Connell's face lit up as soon as the picture was placed before him. He could name every player, every alickadoo, and had a line on all of them. His 19-year-old self is standing in the middle row, with a beaming, enthusiastic smile.

'What do I see? I wish I still had a lot of his qualities,' he said. 'There's a good naivety there. To me, then, rugby was about the physical battle and nothing else – because I knew nothing else because I was taught nothing else. It's not a bad trait to have as a second row, y'know? That Junior

Cup-winning team was the best crack ever. We'd two 30-man brawls in the final against Kilfeacle. Our prop Eddie Fraher got sent off and poor Rosie [Jason Rose], who was our number six, had to come off so we could get another prop on. Just incredible days. Some clubs have philosophies. People talk about the way Garryowen like to keep the ball in hand. In Munsters, all anybody wanted to talk about in the clubhouse was physicality, mauling and making physical statements on the pitch. There wasn't much chat about skill development.'

The importance of the club game to Irish rugby may have diminished since that photo was taken, but O'Connell was convinced that Young Munster was the making of him. There was no Munster Academy back then. His rugby education took place on Tuesday and Thursday nights in Tom Clifford Park, when the junior (second) team would maul and scrummage against the seniors.

'The floodlights wouldn't have been great, they would only have covered a small patch of grass, and we'd be just killing each other,' he said with a gravelly chuckle. 'I wouldn't say the juniors hated the senior team but they were bitter towards them, bitter over the senior coaches for not picking them. I was able to hold my own in those sessions but I wouldn't say I was in a mad rush, really. I had gone back playing rugby at around 16. Rugby hadn't been the sole focus. But winning a Junior Cup became a big ambition. Ger Earls [Keith's dad and O'Connell's boyhood hero] used to always talk about winning the Junior Cup. My dad had played Junior Cup for Young Munsters.

'Those Tuesday nights gave me a great grounding. That edge – it was a habit for me, not something I had to cultivate when I went to Munster U-20s training or Ireland U-20s training. While a guy who had played schools for Blackrock all his life may have had a bigger skill-set than me, I had that edge, because I was living it every Tuesday, Thursday and Saturday. To me, that's what rugby was about.'

And of course, that was still what rugby was about for O'Connell – maintaining that edge even now, in his 36th year. He had to be cute about it, and careful with his body. He'd be out on the training pitch 15 minutes earlier than everyone, to go through an elaborate series of stretches, and he'd factor two or three massages into his plan for each week. Getting out of bed the morning after matches could be hard work, he admitted.

'I was in ribbons after Munster's back-to-back games against Clermont in the Champions Cup,' O'Connell said. 'No injuries, but my shoulders hurt, my neck hurt, my knees hurt. Brendan Grace has a joke where he goes down to tie his laces and he tries to see what other jobs he can get done while he's down there. I can be a bit like that at times. And my ears – they've almost fallen off, with all the cuts. I've had so many stitches at the top, at the join, that the skin isn't very strong.'

But none of this reduced O'Connell's desire to beat the French. Some of his most memorable days have been in France, albeit mainly with Munster – and of course with Emily, with whom he tied the knot in Auch, in the south-west of the country. Since the previous November, there had been stories in the French sports pages about the possibility of O'Connell joining a Top 14 club after the 2015 Rugby World Cup – not that he was giving them any added oxygen. What preoccupied him now was improving a horrendous personal record against Les Bleus: Played 14, won two.

While we're in stat-mode, it's worth pointing out that France's results since the previous World Cup had been awful by their standards. They'd won only 14 of the 33 games they'd played under Philippe Saint-André, who was already seen as a lame duck coach – no one in the French media believed he'd be retained after the World Cup. Remarkably, France had never finished in the top half of the Six Nations table under Saint-André. At the same time, no one in France expected this game to be anything other than tight. How could it be? In the previous six games between the teams, there had been two consecutive draws and an average points differential of 2.66. Whatever about France's results, whatever about their lack of organisation, there was no doubting the individual threats they posed. 'I had the luxury of coaching Wesley Fofana for a few years,' said Schmidt. 'I don't think there are many in world rugby better than him at changing an angle. The try Teddy Thomas scored against Australia shows how you can never rest against France. How do you contain Mathieu Bastareaud?'

Indeed there was a grisly fascination about Bastareaud coming into this game, specifically about him and Sexton, given that one of the Irishman's four concussions had come as a result of a forearm smash by the Toulon wrecking ball in the corresponding game the previous season – *L'histoire d'un bus et d'un pieton*, as one French website put it (like a pedestrian trying to tackle a bus). Just as Benezech predicted, it wasn't very long (seven minutes, to be precise) before Bastareaud was charging up Sexton's channel, only to meet with stiff resistance. 1–0 to Sexton. You just wondered why he insisted on remaining so upright in the tackle. Yes, doing so considerably reduced the threat of the off-load, but Sexton made himself an even bigger, more vulnerable target.

And yet it seems ridiculous to criticise Sexton, given how well he performed after a three-month lay-off. The pinpoint accuracy of his restarts was just one reason that Ireland won the aerial battle, on a day when there was plenty of kicking by both sides. But Sexton out-played Camille Lopez in every phase, and this was one of the main reasons that Ireland won the game, 18–11 – a big margin of victory in the context of those recent results, but still another sweaty, claustrophobic affair with only one try and precious little open rugby, heavily influenced by the referee, Wayne Barnes, who awarded 26 penalties/free kicks and showed two yellow cards over the course of a gruelling 80 minutes. One of those cards was against Rory Best – only the second Irish card during Schmidt's time in charge – and the coach was agitated that the penalty count against his side was in double figures, when they average just seven penalties conceded per Test. Ireland were still more disciplined than their opponents and made the French pay for their lawlessness at the breakdown in particular by successfully converting all six of their kicks at goal, five by Sexton and one by Ian Madigan. Lopez managed just two successes from four attempts, and this was a big deciding factor.

Having been the main story during the build-up, Sexton remained central to the drama, and created a scary new plot-line when he clashed heads with Bastareaud (who else?) five minutes into the second half, at which stage Ireland led 12–6 – in an ironic twist, this time it was the pedestrian running at the bus, rather than the other way around. The possibility of another concussion was too terrible to contemplate, so the ear-splitting roar that greeted Sexton's appearance on the touchline in the 55th minute, six stitches over his left eye but passed fit to continue battle after a 10-minute Head Injury Assessment (HIA), could easily have been a communal sigh of relief.

Madigan had kicked Ireland's lead to 15–6 in the meantime, and now Sexton had the opportunity to put Ireland beyond reach when Conor Murray created an overlap with a darting run off the side of a maul. Maybe it was the shock of finding himself in semi-open country, maybe it was that his vision had been slightly impaired by the swelling above his eye, but Sexton flung his pass to Jared Payne so hard and unsympathetically that it smacked the centre in the face, prompting the rather cruel joke that Payne would need an HIA of his own.

Ireland would have to defend their way to victory instead. They got a raw deal from Barnes, who showed Pascal Papé a yellow card for a nasty knee into Jamie Heaslip's back when he should have shown red – a point acknowledged by the disciplinary panel which subsequently banned the Frenchman for 10 weeks. This wasn't much comfort at the time, when Heaslip had to be replaced and Papé was allowed to return for a tense final quarter. Just to raise the degree of Ireland's difficulty, Best got himself binned for obstruction and while Lopez missed the relatively easy penalty, Barnes chose this stage of the game to start penalising Mike Ross at the scrum – even though Ross had been relatively comfortable up to this point.

As in Paris the previous year, France were well-served by their bench, especially tight-five replacements Atonio, Vincent Debaty and Romain Taofifenua (combined weight 401 kg). With Sexton having kicked Ireland to 18–6 with 13 minutes remaining, France were pressurised into searching for tries. They actually began to play rugby a little truer to their heritage, seeking space rather than contact, and off-loading cleverly. Imagine that! It worked, too, as Taofifenua got on the end of an excellent sequence of running and passing. Lopez missed the conversion but with 10 minutes on the clock, only seven points separated the teams – surely not another draw? But Ireland were familiar with having to defend a lead at home. The Aviva recognised the situation also and weighed in behind the defensive effort, which culminated with Simon Zebo, of all people, bundling Rémi Lamerat into touch to complete the shut-out.

This was Ireland's ninth win on the bounce, prompting Brian O'Driscoll to tweet post-match that a grand slam was on. Schmidt smiled wryly when it was put to him at the post-match press conference. 'That's great of Drico,' he said.

'I was incredibly proud of the defensive display, and that we fought our corner really, particularly when we were a man down in that last quarter. France have some of the biggest humans I have ever seen on a rugby pitch coming at us and it is very, very difficult to arrest their momentum once it begins.

'We have three incredibly tough games left. We get to play at home against England and that is monumental for us. A slam? That's for later on because I think it could all come undone right here, next match. We've managed to build a bit of a home record [this was the seventh straight home win] and I know the players take incredible pride playing here at the Aviva. We've had fantastic support. I know myself I have had a number of people putting pressure on me to see if I can find England tickets for them. It has been sold out for a long time. It's going to be a massive occasion and we won't be looking past that.'

The news on Heaslip would take some gloss off the victory – it emerged that he had suffered fractures of the transverse process of three verte-brae in his back. Schmidt would also have to sweat further over Sexton's well-being, seeing as Racing needed him to play the following Saturday, when everyone else would be taking the weekend off. Not that Sexton was trying to avoid action. Quite the opposite.

'Well I need game time, don't I?' Sexton said on the night of the France game. 'I've been away for 12 weeks and I did feel a bit rusty at times tonight, so I think I'll be better with another 50 or 60 minutes. I'm mad keen to get back and get some more game time under my belt.'

Sexton revealed that he'd had no concussion concerns when he was removed for an HIA. He'd only been worried that his eye might close over. 'I got slit one time before and I couldn't really see out of that side but it didn't happen this time,' Sexton said. 'The doctors did a great job and I was fine. Head-wise I felt great. I was really happy. I was almost pleased to get a bang like that so it proves to myself there is no issue going forward. It's just great to put it to bed now.'

Sexton had been as bemused as his coach by the comments of Monsieur Benezech, as reported by the *Irish Times*. 'Yeah, Joe had a word with me about it yesterday,' said Sexton. 'He couldn't really believe it. I'd been out of the game for 12 weeks. One guy said that I shouldn't play because Bastareaud is playing? Well, then I can never play because next week I'm going to have to play against Fritz Lee; the week after I'll have to play against Luther Burrell and Billy Vunipola. It's absolute stupidity to say that I shouldn't play because Bastareaud was playing. Joe gets told by the doctors who is fit and who's not and I don't know why he got brought into it by this fella who seems to have an opinion on everything.'

As for O'Connell, you can be sure that it took him a while to remove his body from the bed the next morning; that he was stiff and sore but happy after only his third victory over France. He knew his record against England was a bit better – seven wins, three losses – though he wouldn't be shouting about this. This England side were worthy of respect, as always. 'Even when England went through that bad period after winning the World Cup in 2003, it was always an incredibly hard, bruising game against them,' he told me. 'This team seems to have all the right values. They're really hungry, really fit, really disciplined and well-organised. Then they still have that physical edge as well. This is going to be up another level.'

IRELAND 18, FRANCE 11
AVIVA STADIUM, 14 FEBRUARY 2015

Ireland: R Kearney; T Bowe, J Payne, R Henshaw, S Zebo; J Sexton (I Madigan 45–55), C Murray; J McGrath (C Healy 63), R Best (S Cronin 72), M Ross (M Moore 63); D Toner (I Henderson, 75), P O'Connell (capt); P O'Mahony, S O'Brien (Cronin 66–72), J Heaslip (J Murphy 60).
Sinbinned: Best (61–71 mins).

France: S Spedding (R Talès 53); Y Huget, M Bastareaud (Talès 45–53), W Fofana (R Lamerat 14–23), T Thomas (Lamerat 33); C Lopez, R Kockott (M Parra 68); E Ben Arous (V Debaty 51), G Guirado (B Kayser 51), R Slimani (U Atonio 51); P Papé (R Taofifenua 62), Y Maestri; T Dusautoir (capt), B le Roux, D Chouly (L Gougon 72).
Sinbinned: Papé (53–63 mins).

Referee: Wayne Barnes (England).

Scoring sequence: 14 mins: Sexton pen 3–0; 16 mins: Lopez pen 3–3; 19 mins: Sexton pen 6–3; 33 mins: Sexton pen 9–3; 36 mins: Lopez pen 9–6; 39 mins: Sexton pen 12–6; 51 mins: Madigan pen 15–6; 68 mins: Sexton pen 18–6; 71 mins: Taofifenua try 18–11.

9

ENGLAND: AILIS EGAN

Kate Rowan

Move over 'bromance': it is all about the 'fromance' now! It is not a difficult concept to understand. Think the same sort of tightly bonded friendship as the dudes in a 'bromance' share, except that this is the unique relationship of the members of Ireland's women's front row. One of the women at the centre of the 'fromance' is tight-head prop Ailis Egan. Ailis has the sort of dedication, focus and ambition for her sport that would almost leave you breathless. She is also an extremely articulate history graduate of Trinity College Dublin. Yet she is incredibly bubbly and at times possesses an almost girlish enthusiasm for the *craic* of playing alongside her best friends. And that is the kernel of what 'fromance' is about: it is about training like a professional while your sport is still amateur, but it is also about a deep-rooted camaraderie that comes from playing in some of the more mysterious positions on the rugby field.

With an air of faux martyrdom and a cheeky chuckle, 31-year-old Egan – whose day job is in fundraising administration for MS Ireland – speaks of how the toils of the front row are often misunderstood: 'We would joke about the backs, how they are useless ... without us they would not get the ball and they would not get the space to score their amazing tries. There is a big banter in terms of that. We would slag them, saying "You don't know what a scrum is like", and ... we would slag Briggsy [Niamh Briggs] or Jenny [Murphy] for getting the media attention.'

Joking aside, there is some truth in this: the media does tend to give extra attention to our backline stars. While covering the men's game, I have noticed that notwithstanding many journalists' studious and well-informed questioning of the likes of Mike Ross on the finer points of scrummaging, a significant number seem disproportionately focused on backs. Many fans in Ireland have converted to rugby only in the past 10 or 15 years; to some the scrum seems somewhat perplexing. Having grown up surrounded by Gaelic football and soccer, they may have a better sense of understanding and empathy with the backs. So, it could be argued, when it comes to selling newspapers or generating hits on a website, backs in Ireland have greater popular appeal than the front row. In contrast, in New Zealand, where the majority of the population have been raised on rugby, understanding and appreciation of the front row is innate. During my two visits to the Land of the Long White Cloud – to cover the 2011 Rugby World Cup and Ireland's ill-fated three-Test tour against the All Blacks the following year – much of the media and local fan interest concerning Ireland centred on our loose-head Cian Healy, dubbed a 'rock star prop' by his Kiwi admirers.

Then there is the simple truth that it is difficult to fully comprehend the intricacies of propping unless you have stood in the front row. Bearing that in mind, I decided that if we are to give our props and hookers – both female and male – the love they deserve in Ireland, those of us looking on to the pitch from the stands need a lesson. For this, there is no better woman than Egan.

Let's start with the easy stuff: part of the reason for the strong bond between herself, hooker Gillian Bourke and props Ruth O'Reilly and Fiona Hayes, she believes, is that 'the front row is very different; there is a lot of trust and working together and relying on each other. You spend an awful lot of time together ... you develop great relationships. My best friends are pretty much the guys in the front row.'

For those of us yet to experience scrummaging at international level, what does it physically feel like to be a tight-head, driving the scrum? 'As a tight-head all the pressure is coming in onto your side. Physically it is one of the most draining things you will ever do. For however amount of seconds it is, it feels like the longest time known to man – if you are on top it's brilliant.' At the thought of getting one over on her opposition, Egan becomes even more animated: 'If you are on top ... you think you are a massive man mountain and you are king of the world and you are beasting everyone.' After that spurt of enthusiasm, her demeanour changes to seeming almost exhausted: 'but it is so, so tiring. At 60 minutes plus in a game, if you have done a lot of scrums, over and over again, it is physically exhausting, especially if you are under pressure. If you are scrummaging against France or England there is huge amount of pressure and if you get it wrong it's the difference between winning and losing a game.'

In the 2015 Six Nations Championship, Egan, Bourke and O'Reilly were facing the toughest scrummaging sides in France and England back to back. Although it is over two months later when I speak to her, her exasperation at the loss is still apparent: 'God, France. That is definitely one that got away from us. The first half was all about France and we were lucky to hold them out. The second half was all ours, we were all over them but we didn't convert it. I scored a try and I thought we would kick on and win that game. We were inches from their line. There was that overlap and we should have won that game. You live and learn and move on. Game management had to be a little bit better. Execution had to be better and we learned from that going into England. From a forward's perspective we had to get our attack in the green zone better, and it was.'

Going into the third round of Six Nations matches, both Ireland and England had won and lost a game, so it was a crucial match. Ireland were hoping to atone for the 40–7 beating the English inflicted on them six months previously in the World Cup semi-final in Paris. The only change to the starting 15 from the France match was the return of Hannah Tyrrell after recovering from concussion. In the build-up, Egan and her tight-five colleagues could see some potential weaknesses in the World Champion Red Roses' pack: 'We knew they were missing their big guns but from a forward's perspective, the front five were the same front five that were in the World Cup bar the fact they had two key retirements, Sophie Hemming and Jo McGilchrist, world-class tight-head and world-class second row. I knew as a tight five we could attack them. The media would probably have never picked up on that but that was probably a bigger loss for them than them missing the likes of backs Emily Scarratt and Rachel Burford and all of those. At the end of the day the forward platform is where your ball is coming from. They were a pack in transition whereas we weren't. Bar Ruth [O'Reilly] replacing Fiona [Coghlan], we had been together as a starting eight for a good two or three years.'

The head-to-head battles are another unique aspect of the front row: 'It is probably the only area of the pitch you have a one-on-one battle. 10s and 12s are up against each other but you don't have that proximity. If the loose-head gets one up on me, she has won. You are basically spending each scrum trying to figure each other out and trying to outdo the other one.' This sparked a memory of an interview with Irish hooker Rory Best during the 2012 tour to New Zealand. Best spoke about regarding his All Black counterpart Andrew Hore with the same sort of familiarity as would have existed if Best was working in a company's Belfast office and Hore was an Auckland-based colleague. It wasn't exactly friendly, but there was a professional intimacy when each player described how the other worked that I had not noticed previously, except with props. Egan explains, however, that the situation 'is a bit different for the men because they play each other more often but this being my fourth year, it is the first time I actually [think] "Ah I know this person, I know how they scrummage and I know what to do."' When veteran English loose-head Rochelle Clark comes up, Egan refers to her using her nickname 'Rocky' with the same sort of familiarity that her male counterparts would use.

This level of professional acquaintanceship comes from the fact that, according to Egan, 'You spend all your time studying them. You would be sitting there for an hour or two, looking at your opposite number scrum-maging, how they scrummage, what are their weaknesses, where you can attack them. Year on year you are up against the same people so you do get to know them.' This can lead to a rather incongruous form of chit-chat in the heat of battle: 'There is a bit of banter. It can be chatty and it depends on the language barriers, but every so often you would have a laugh if some-thing is going on.' Then, returning to more serious matters: 'Mentally, it is one of the toughest positions because if it is going wrong, it is all on you. For me in the World Cup, against France, there was a scrum down in our five-metre line and loose-head got under me, our scrum was destroyed, they got a penalty, they kicked the points and went ahead. When I was standing underneath those posts, I never felt so lonely in my life. I was thinking, 'That was all down to me.' I would always blame myself ... [if] you have had that one-on-one battle and you have lost, it's just such a horrible, horrible feeling.'

So, Egan's position takes a unique mental and physical toll, and 'our training is very different. When you are training, coaching and trying to teach people about scrums, it is alien.' These factors combine to create a sense of almost a sisterhood in arms. Of all the players I spoke to, Egan's story had the strongest feeling of herself and teammates going into battle warrior-like. In contrast, she describes a very nurturing environment to train and play in: 'The girls see you at your lowest and support you through horrendous personal times. My dad had a stroke at Christmas just before the Grand Slam year. He's doing brilliantly now, but ... that whole Six Nations was horrendous for me. I don't know what I would have done without the girls because they got me through it. I remember one day I was doing my weights, but just crying at the same time. They don't do anything. They are just there for you. I guess they didn't make a show of me, but carried on, got me talking about something different, distracted me. Another example – after the World Cup, myself and my partner broke up. I rang up Gillian and she was there within four hours. She drove all the way from Cork, straight up to Dublin.' Egan, Bourke and Hayes also enjoyed a trip to New York together as a treat after the World Cup, which they described as 'Fromance on tour'. The contrast between having 'an innate aggression', which generally is perceived as a masculine trait, and this sense of female friendships really helps to challenge stereotypes around women in sport.

It was Egan's father Sean, formerly CEO of Aviva Ireland, who encouraged his daughter to pick up a rugby ball before she left the family home in Bath for her studies in Dublin. Although raised in England, she grew up in a very Irish home, 'always identifying as Irish': her paternal grandparents hailed from County Tipperary. Ailis is the eldest in a family of four; she and sisters Niamh and Ciar were born within four years of each other, with a nine-year-gap until brother Ruairí arrived. With great pride she describes her mother Morag, a French and German teacher, as 'staunchly feminist' – 'I grew up in a house without gender stereotypes.' She speaks of 'running around with swords', play-fighting and playing games of 'Mercy' with her siblings, and her father organising sprint races between the family, 'so rugby came as second nature'. Egan was never tempted to play for the Red Roses, having made Dublin her permanent home after her studies in Trinity.

When game day arrives, although Egan must often fend off a fit of giggles at 'fromance' pal O'Reilly's off-key rendition of 'Ireland's Call', during those precious moments before battle she often thinks about her family, particularly since her father's recovery from stroke: 'Nobody knows what rehab is until you have a stroke. You see what he did in rehab. If anyone ever complains about an injury I'm just: "Really? Learn to walk again." He is back to working a few days a week and back to himself.' She sees Sean and Morag as 'Huge, important figures in my life. I would think about them before games. They are inspirational.'

Ireland's final home fixture of their campaign was do or die as far as Egan and her team-mates were concerned: 'Losing to France was a big blow but winning against England was absolutely essential. Otherwise our campaign was dead in the water.'

England opened the evening's scoring as World Cup winning captain and out-half Katy McLean slotted an 11th-minute close-range penalty.

The Irish restored parity when Briggs successfully kicked a penalty. In terms of tries, the English again had the first say as number 8 Harriet Millar-Mills crashed over in the closing moments of the first half, on the back of a powerful scrum. How this score was conceded particularly disappointed Egan, and months later it still haunts her: 'From a forward's perspective, their try was from a scrum. It went backwards on our five-metre line. It is something that Gill and I had spoken about on so many occasions. We never wanted it to happen and it happened. It happened in the [World Cup] semi-final and this year. It is something that we will again look at. We will go back to the drawing board and try to fix it. But it is something that really, really rankles with myself and Gill that we allowed them to do that to us again. That try wasn't because they were superior to us in terms of strength. They manipulated us and manipulated the wheel. We weren't clued in and focused enough, as we should have been.'

The hosts were re-energised after the interval, and spent 10 minutes camped in English territory. A try from Larissa Muldoon on the 50-minute mark broke the terrific English defence. Briggs missed the conversion. In the dying moments Ireland were awarded a penalty for England coming in at the side of a ruck. Having received treatment for cramp, Briggs took the kick and snatched a famous victory that kept Ireland in contention for the Six Nations title.

Despite the victory, Egan's self-critical nature comes to the fore again: 'It was closer than I would have liked. I didn't feel at all during the game that we were going to lose, but Briggsy got the penalty that pulled us away and allowed us to win. I didn't think we weren't going to win, but it was closer than it should have been. We should have been further ahead.'

This was only the second time in their history that Ireland's women had beaten the English – the other occasion was during 2013's grand slam season. Egan's discontent with how her side played, despite their victory, says everything you need to know about the Class of 2015.

IRELAND 11, ENGLAND 8
MILLTOWN HOUSE, ASHBOURNE RFC
27 FEBRUARY 2015

Ireland: N Briggs (capt); H Tyrrell, J Murphy, K Fitzhenry, A Miller; N Stapleton, L Muldoon (T Rosser 71); R O'Reilly (F Hayes 48), G Bourke, A Egan (Fiona O'Brien 80+5); S Spence, ML Reilly; P Fitzpatrick, C Molloy, H O'Brien.

England: L Cattell (H Field 79); R Laybourn (A Reed 76), A Brown (M Goddard 80), C Large, S Gregson; K McLean (capt), B Blackburn (F Davidson 80); R Clark, V Fleetwood, L Keates; T Taylor, A Scott; A Matthews, H Gallagher, H Millar-Mills.

Referee: L Berard (USA).

Scoring sequence: 11 mins: McLean pen 0–3; 25 mins: Briggs pen 3–3; 40 mins: Millar-Mills try 3–8; 50 mins: Muldoon try 8–8; 80 mins: Briggs pen 11–8.

10

ENGLAND: ROBBIE HENSHAW

Peter O'Reilly

D-Day in Dublin. Title decider. Grand slam play-off. Such descriptions seemed a little premature, given that we were only halfway through the tournament and that Wales had launched something of a comeback by winning in Edinburgh and Paris, but there was a special hum of antici-pation around Dublin 4 on Sunday, 1 March. Coming into Round Three, Ireland and England were the only unbeaten sides and the bookmakers could barely separate them – for the record, Ireland went in as one-point favourites on the spread. The Aviva would be heaving.

Ireland had momentum, certainly, and playing at home was an advantage again, after a difficult teething period for the new stadium – the team was aiming for its eighth straight win here. A few doubts niggled away at supporters, however. Could Ireland win the breakdown battle without Jamie Heaslip? Would Joe Marler do a number on Mike Ross at the scrum, as he had done for Harlequins against Leinster in the Champions Cup? And how were Ireland going to score tries? They had scored only two so far in the championship, both against a 14-man Italy, and neither of which had been the product of any special invention. Yes, they had crossed both Australia and South Africa's try-line twice, but again, they had been prosaic tries – Simon Zebo or Tommy Bowe chasing a kick or picking off an interception, Rhys Ruddock being driven over at the line-out. For some, the notion that England played more attractive rugby than Ireland was a little hard to take.

Under Schmidt, Ireland had become the essence of functionality – solid set-piece, impregnable defence and brilliant kick-chase. One of the images of the championship thus far had been of Bowe chasing a Sexton restart against France, just to see the impressive height of his spring – it looked as though his feet were a couple of metres off the turf. It was high-pressure, low-risk rugby, based on accurate execution. Give Ireland a lead and they'd be almost impossible to haul in. But what if Ireland had to do the hauling? What if they had to pull a rabbit from the hat? We'd seen the pyrotechnics that Schmidt had stage-managed with Leinster, those beautifully choreographed attacking power-plays. We waited for him to dip into his catalogue with Ireland, and he did so to some extent – but not this season. Risk had been removed from the equation. Build pressure, force errors, take your points. Shut-up-shop rugby, as it was memorably called by Alan Gaffney, Ireland's attack coach under Declan Kidney.

There had been a remarkable stat from the South Africa game – zero off-loads by Ireland. In the modern game, where specialist defence coaches appear to have shrunk the rugby pitch, clean breaks become rarer and rarer. Passing out of the tackle offers a more likely means of cracking the defensive line, but Schmidt didn't seem to like the element of risk – especially after Zebo attempted an off-load against the Wallabies and the end result was a Nick Phipps try at the other end of the pitch. He'd rather quick, clean, and secure ruck ball than the risk of a turnover.

We asked Schmidt about this after the November Tests and he said that off-loading was an aspiration for him – but only when the team was ready. 'To be able to play on your feet is advantageous, without a doubt,' he said. 'But we had so many different combinations during the autumn, especially with making 13 changes for the Georgia game [between the South Africa and Australia Tests], so to be able to know where people are running to and coming from and getting that almost intuitive sense of where your support player is, is difficult.

'One of the things about the World Cup is that we'll have an extended lead-up together when we can build combinations, which is when you can be effective at off-loading. I don't have a hang-up about it. I wouldn't even say I have a rugby philosophy. I just think that you try to maximise the resources you have currently available and the combinations that they form, and if those combinations are newly formed I do think to play in a particular fashion becomes more difficult.'

In other words, Brian O'Driscoll could flick one-handed passes out the back to Gordon d'Arcy, because they'd played together at the highest level for over a decade; Robbie Henshaw and Jared Payne haven't even played much at centre, let alone played at centre together. What's more, there's not much point in setting up plays for dynamic ball-carriers if the Sean O'Briens and Cian Healys are only on their way back to playing. It's called cutting your cloth, or coaching flexibility, and it's one of the reasons that Schmidt has been so successful.

That people would fail to see that logic clearly irked him a little, especially when he was asked on the eve of the England game about Ireland being tagged as 'one-dimensional' or being branded as 'a kick-chase team'.

'I am not too aware of how we are perceived,' Schmidt said, 'but I know we have kicked less than some other teams in the championship and if people have a look they might find it is our opponents at the weekend who have kicked the most.'

This took people slightly by surprise, for it was not how this England team was perceived. After decades of being branded as 'boring', especially by folks south of the equator, England now had pace out wide and weren't afraid to use it – they'd scored eight tries in two games. One person above all had lit up the tournament and was already being hyped as a star for England's very own World Cup: Jonathan Joseph.

'He's the first bloke to really get the English pulse going after a 10-year hiatus,' said Stuart Barnes, the former England out-half, now a pundit with Sky Sports and the *Sunday Times*. 'We've had a sterile midfield and become obsessed with size, with running into people instead of beating them with speed. Joseph's got speed and that incredible footwork. He can draw defenders towards him then speeds away, leaving them standing, as if they've been turned to stone. It lifts the crowd. It's elegant and it's exciting and English rugby has been neither elegant nor exciting for years.'

Will Greenwood, another former England international, positively gushed as he described Joseph's try against Wales in the Millennium: 'Dan Biggar charges him and he feints in and out, feet in control, like the guy from *The Matrix*, swaying and dodging. He sees North and Rhys Webb, realises he needs a stronger platform, the tippy tappy feet stop and he drops into wider base, lower body angles. He rides the hit and goes in and under, before finding free space. And once he has that, he is almost instantly into a normal stride almost as if he was jogging in the park rather than delivering a blow to Wales in their mighty stadium, and sending a message to England supporters that they might well have a new Jeremy Guscott.'

You had the impression that England needed a new star, especially in Rugby World Cup year. George Ford had been impressive since taking over the number 10 jersey from Owen Farrell, had offered something different in attack and also had star quality. But Joseph made good copy too.

Not only did he look like Guscott and play for the same club – Bath – but there were other interesting angles to his story. He was on something of a comeback trail, having been capped three times as a 21-year-old in South Africa in 2012 only to disappear completely from view. Stuart Lancaster hadn't even selected him to tour New Zealand in the summer of 2014 but now his club form had made him an exciting alternative to the injured Manu Tuilagi. Schmidt had recognised the threat Joseph posed by designating Keith Earls as his 'body double' for the entire two weeks leading up to the England game, as Earls's footwork most closely resembled the Englishman's.

Schmidt's Ireland weren't so much about star quality as the cult of the team; about 'brutal functionality', as someone described their methods. However, the team's shirt sponsors were in no doubt as to whom they wanted centre-stage in their Six Nations ad campaign. Sexton would be there, obviously; so too the skipper, O'Connell. But Robbie Henshaw was their new poster boy, a new O'Driscoll if you like – so much so that they rigged him out in a smouldering green number 13 jersey, even though Schmidt had decided that the team would be better served with the burly 21-year-old at 12.

If Joseph had carried more ball than any England player thus far, Henshaw had stopped most opponents for Ireland – their top tackler against Italy (15) and France (16). He was built for such work, too: significantly bigger than his predecessors at 1.91 metres tall and weighing in at 100 kilos. No wonder Warren Gatland, the man who brought gigantic three-quarter lines into vogue in the northern hemisphere, once asked Henshaw whether he qualified to play for Wales. No wonder Henshaw's favourite player growing up was that purveyor of pain, Tana Umaga. The 12-year-old Henshaw so revered the former All Blacks captain that he even approached him at Lansdowne Road, at a time when Umaga was actively avoiding attention.

'It was 2005, after the O'Driscoll incident,' Henshaw once told me. 'I met him in the stand with my dad. I was really fascinated by him, so I was kind of nervous meeting him. I think he was right not to play that day. The crowd would have given him an awful going over.'

This was the first time I'd met Henshaw, in December 2013, and we were sitting in the offices at the Sportsground in Galway. The previous summer, he'd become only the sixth born-and-bred Connacht man to have been capped for Ireland in the professional era, when he'd played full-back against the American Eagles in Houston. He'd marked the occasion by singing 'Galway Girl' at the top of the team bus. Here was a 20-year-old who was clearly in touch with his roots – his musical roots in particular.

'Yeah, I play a little bit of trad,' he said. 'That's something that's been in my family for years. My granddad, Billy Henshaw, he started it all. As kids, we'd go up to him and he'd whistle into our ears and we'd try and play back what he heard. My first instrument was the fiddle and then I moved on to the accordion. I haven't performed much recently but a couple of years back, every weekend, I used to perform in local pubs, with my dad and cousins, just trad sessions, good crack.'

The confidence to perform in front of bigger crowds was slower in coming. Eric Elwood was the first to pronounce Henshaw as a star in the making, picking him for Connacht the year he left Marist College in Athone. 'He just kept in my ear, encouraging me,' said Henshaw. 'His main line to me was: "If you're good enough you're old enough. Don't worry about your age. Just do what you normally do and do what you have been doing and you'll be able to succeed at this standard."'

Schmidt was so convinced of Henshaw's readiness for international rugby that he'd been ready to pitch him in against the All Blacks, had O'Driscoll not been declared fit to play late in the day. And while Henshaw didn't play a single minute of the 2014 Six Nations, he was 24th man for all five games and hungry for every crumb of information and help that O'Driscoll could provide.

'He was invaluable for me, as one-to-one coach and as mentor,' said Henshaw. 'We'd chat over coffee or sit down at the laptop and go through things. Even after he retired, he'd send me texts, give me the good and the bad of a game, how I did and what I could improve on. He was a genius at most things in the game, and he went through lines of attack, lines in defence, when to come up hard off the line and when to hold back and just not bite in. Things like that and just a bit of passing skills. We used to do one-on-one passing and stuff like that after training. All parts of the game he would help me with.

Gordon D'Arcy proved similarly generous-spirited, even after Henshaw had been selected ahead of him for the South Africa Test the previous

November. 'Darce said: "If you can play 13 you can play 12." It's just one slot in, just do the same things and stay connected with your 10 and your 13. There's a good side to it. I can run physical hard lines and I can try and put in some big hits whereas there's more traffic coming down the way. That's a positive that I will be taking out of it, that I can possibly gear up for putting in some massive tackles.'

With all those positive influences from O'Driscoll and D'Arcy, and with Henshaw apparently hugely enthusiastic about his time spent in camp with Johnny Sexton, it was probably no surprise that people started talking about the possibility of a move to Leinster, even though Henshaw was contracted until the end of the 2015/16 season. It wasn't just chat, either – the player himself had explored the possibility of moving ahead of time. So you can imagine how he felt when Schmidt called a training session against Connacht at the Sportsground the week before the England game. Here he was, the only Connacht player in an Ireland squad densely populated by Leinstermen, going head-to-head with his provincial teammates in a practice game, played before a crowd of 3,000 adoring schoolkids on their mid-term break. 'It was a bit different, all right. I haven't been back in Galway for a while so it was good to go against the lads. There was a little bit of niggle there as well,' he chuckled.

Nothing like as much niggle as you tend to get in games against England, however. Ireland were full to the brim of motivational fuel, having lost four in a row to the Red Rose, including the previous two times the sides had met at the Aviva. Schmidt added a drop of vinegar to the mix by declaring that beating England would be the biggest win of his time as Ireland coach.

Certainly, it turned out to be one of the most accurate performances by any Irish side, a ruthless and relentless hunting down of an England team that looked a collective couple of years too young to be backing themselves as World Cup contenders, even on their own patch. Yes, Ireland scored just one try and, as the style police were quick to point out, they kicked the ball 44 times from the hand. But Sexton and Murray kicked so accurately, and the chasers chased so furiously and contested so hungrily, that Ireland got to dominate territory (58%) and possession (59%). There was the odd occasion when Alex Goode or Anthony Watson evaded the first chase-line and skipped daringly into open territory, but they were hunted down, and danger was smothered emphatically.

On a bitingly cold afternoon, Ireland simply froze England out, in just about every phase. And they did it from the start. If ever there was a statement of intent, it was the way Sexton spotted Ford hiding on the left touchline and dropped a bomb on him – a bomb that came with a welcoming party in Tommy Bowe, who forced the turnover. Ireland brought that perfect blend of fury and precision and England simply gave away penalties – two of them in the first eight minutes, to give Ireland the ideal opening.

Ford did drop a neat goal to register England's presence on the scoreboard, but not all of his decision-making was smart. Approaching half-time, he tried to run the ball out of his own 22 only to be mugged by

Sexton, who drilled him into the dirt and then celebrated wildly – perhaps too wildly, for when Ford was penalised for holding on, Sexton pulled the kick to the left. His first miss of the championship.

It barely mattered, for Ireland were winning all the battles, collective and individual. At the scrum, Ford quietly put Marler back in his place. When England dared to kick to the corner in the second quarter Devin Toner pinched the throw and England regretted their decision. Ireland dominated in the air and they dominated on the turf – despite losing Sean O'Brien to concussion in the 25th minute. Tommy O'Donnell deputised manfully and Jordi Murphy made light of Heaslip's absence with a performance that was half superhero, half Duracell Bunny. All told, Ireland had a remarkable ruck efficiency rate of just under 99 per cent – 116 won, just two lost – which was as clinical as they'd ever been.

Above all, it was a victory for work-rate, as could be seen in the build-up to Henshaw's try. For it was Zebo – supposedly languid and lackadaisical – who forced a turnover in England's 22 by harrying Watson and then flipping him over in a judo throw. As Ireland kept possession through the phases, you noticed the likes of Tommy Bowe flying into the rucks, another wing willing to do the dirty work. Even the try itself, while it looked off the cuff, proved to be something that Henshaw and Conor Murray had rehearsed. 'I spotted the space in behind Alex Goode and I just backed myself,' said Henshaw. 'I caught Conor's eye – I didn't go too mad in case I'd give it away. We had practised it a couple of times, where if we did have a penalty advantage we would possibly put in a kick over the top and have someone chase it. I just happened to be there and gave the nod to Conor to put it in behind and thankfully got on the end of it.'

The English press, in particular, ascribed Ireland's aerial superiority to the number of backs who had played Gaelic football. While Henshaw had, indeed, represented Westmeath at minor level, this wasn't in fact a Gaelic-style catch, above the head. He did 'dominate the space', however, and showed real athleticism to ground the ball before going out of play. As the TMO had to double-check this fact, Irish supporters got to celebrate the try not once or twice, but three times. They could also celebrate the fact that after Sexton's touchline conversion, Ireland led by the faintly ridiculous score of 19–3, with 53 minutes on the clock.

It seemed inconceivable that a team of England's abilities would leave without making a mark of some sort. Sure enough, Sexton departed almost immediately, having tweaked his hamstring in kicking that conversion and in his absence, the visitors enjoyed their period of dominance, which was reflected on the scoreboard by two Ford penalties. But at no stage did the Aviva feel really threatened, in the way that it had done towards the end of the France game. And at no stage, incidentally, did Jonathan Joseph get to imprint his personality on the contest. Ireland remained two scores ahead – a satisfying outcome for Schmidt, given that Ireland played the final quarter with Murphy, O'Donnell and Madigan, all fringe players at the start of the campaign, operating in the middle five.

As for Henshaw, he was an obvious choice for man of the match, not merely because he'd scored the only try of the game but because he'd defended like a devil again, topping the tackle-count for the third game running, this time with 14. 'And they are top-quality tackles as well,' said Schmidt afterwards. 'Robbie is an incredibly understated kid. He is quietly spoken. He just gets on and delivers on the pitch; you really saw that today.'

Ireland had won their 10th straight Test, equalling a record set 12 seasons previously. Stuart Lancaster bemoaned England's lack of discipline – they conceded 13 penalties to Ireland's eight – but was otherwise at a loss to explain how his team had been so emphatically shut out. He and his coaching team had known how Ireland would play but they had been utterly unable to counteract the Schmidt plan. Lancaster could only remain optimistic that Wales could reopen the championship by beating Ireland in Cardiff two weekends later. 'There are so few grand slams,' he said. 'In the majority of seasons, the Six Nations winner loses a game along the way. We have two games at home and it's critical that we get as much as we can out of those. Ireland have two games away and Wales are obviously still in the hunt. We'll see.'

As for Schmidt, he admitted that it was nice to watch an end-game with the security of a 10-point cushion. With all of 13 days to go before Cardiff, he was going to just enjoy the victory for once, to try and put it out of his mind that the slam was still on, and that Ireland were on course to win consecutive titles for the first time in 66 years.

'For once I didn't have my heart in my mouth,' he said. 'I'm not going to think about going forward for another 24 hours. I'm just going to enjoy this 24 hours. I snuck home last night to read a bedtime story to my son, Luke. He was pumped for the game because as long as we win he doesn't have to do homework and so he is a massive Irish supporter as a result! We're a pretty grounded bunch and you stay pretty grounded, but at the same time you do get a little bit excited. It's exciting to have beaten England, it's exciting to be in the position we are in. You don't look at history because you can't necessarily affect history; once it's there, it's there. But you try to influence what is coming in the immediate future.'

IRELAND 19, ENGLAND 9
AVIVA STADIUM, 1 MARCH 2015

Ireland: R Kearney; T Bowe, J Payne (F Jones 71), R Henshaw, S Zebo; J Sexton (I Madigan 54), C Murray; J McGrath (C Healy 59), R Best (S Cronin 74), M Ross (M Moore 58); D Toner (I Henderson 65), P O'Connell; P O'Mahony, S O'Brien (T O'Donnell 25), J Murphy.

ENGLAND: A Goode; A Watson, J Joseph (B Twelvetrees 68), L Burrell, J Nowell; G Ford, B Youngs (R Wigglesworth 68); J Marler (M Vunipola 66), D Hartley (T Youngs 54), D Cole; D Attwood (N Easter 68), G Kruis; J Haskell (T Croft 62), C Robshaw, B Vunipola.

Referee: Craig Joubert (South Africa).

Scoring sequence: 2 mins: Sexton pen 3–0; 9 mins: Sexton pen 6–0; 12 mins: Ford pen 6–3; 30 mins: Sexton pen 9–3; 48 mins: Sexton pen 12–3; 53 mins: Henshaw try, Sexton con 19–3; 59 mins: Ford pen 19–6; 68 mins: Ford pen 19–9.

11

WALES: PAULA FITZPATRICK

Kate Rowan

Ireland's women's back row are not just handy around the breakdown; they would also be able to help out in a medical emergency. Dr Claire Molloy, a medical doctor, is the class of 2015's openside, while number 8 Heather O'Brien is a physiotherapist and blindside flanker Paula Fitzpatrick PhD is an exercise physiologist. If playing rugby for their country and balancing successful careers isn't enough, these three can also bust a mean Beyoncé-style shoulder shimmy.

When I meet Fitzpatrick, who hails from Tallaght, at the labs in Dublin City University where STRIVE – the company she is co-founder and CEO of – is based, she takes me on a tour of the facility. There are numerous treadmills and exercise bikes hooked up to monitors and computers. It all looks very high-tech and slightly mind-boggling, so I decide to draw on the experience of the one place I have seen such a set-up before. In RTE's 2013 documentary *Tommy Bowe's Bodycheck*, the Ireland and Ulster wing underwent a battery of tests similar to those that Fitzpatrick conducts in order to explain how science can help athletes fine-tune their performances. Unfortunately, I didn't remember the full name of the television programme, and blurted out, 'Oh wow, this is just like Tommy Bowe's body!', hoping to show Fitzpatrick that I had at least some sort of crude understanding of her work. She burst out laughing – 'Oh, so you liked Tommy Bowe's *body?*' – and with that I could absolutely imagine herself, Molloy and O'Brien doing their dance routine to 'All The Single Ladies' – of which I had heard much from speaking to their teammates. I had previously found it hard to reconcile the idea of Fitzpatrick, Molloy and O'Brien as serious athletes, who put in some wonderfully gutsy performances in this Six Nations campaign and have equally serious careers, with their being such giddy goats: 'The front row have Fromance; the back-row are always singing "All the Single Ladies"!' And that is what makes Fitzpatrick such a likeable character: she works extremely hard at her rugby and in her lab but she has a great sense of fun, as well as being humble and self-deprecating.

STRIVE is an 'athlete testing and research centre. We have the testing side of things where we get the athletes from all different sports coming in. Then we have the research side of things. That would be where we would complete research of products.' The athlete testing aspect involves working with athletes from team sports including Gaelic games, soccer and rugby, as well as endurance athletes such as triathletes and distance runners, and also canoeists and kayakers. It is not all about Olympic hopefuls, aspiring inter-county stars and rugby and soccer internationals, though, as Fitzpatrick sees her fair share of weekend warriors looking to add an edge to their performance as well as elite-level sportsmen and women. She explains how she works: 'When somebody comes in, we would carry out a needs analysis on what their sport is and what they are looking to achieve. Then we would carry out sports-specific tests to give them an idea of what their strengths and weaknesses might be and what they might need to work on and improve.' The other aspect of STRIVE is the research: 'We did some work for STATSports, the GPS company and … we have worked with a couple of sports drinks … We run basic tests and give them scientific based evidence support for what they are trying to market.'

Why did the 29-year-old Fitzpatrick want to become a scientist in the first place? There is a lovely simplicity to the answer: 'Growing up, I was just interested in how things worked and how to improve them. I didn't even know it was science.' This brought me back to an interview where Jamie Heaslip spoke of how he felt that part of the reason he could do his job so well in Ireland and Leinster's back rows was having an 'engineer's mind'; he, like Fitzpatrick, is a graduate of DCU (in medical mechanical engineering), and felt that his technical or scientific way of analysing situations helped him in reading breakdowns and lineouts. Fitzpatrick, as another back row, agrees. 'Heather and myself would spend a lot of time doing video analysis … we like to be prepared [for] what is coming. If you are informed about something you can anticipate what is going to happen, or what the opposition might do. We do a lot of analysis on them. The video analysts run away from us because we are always after a laptop! Katie Norris works in events but she is very methodical about things as well.'

However, Fitzpatrick wasn't always a flanker. When she was first capped for Ireland in 2012 it was as a hooker; before that, when she was called into Leinster's training squad, she was an outhalf, but the coach at the time – Dan van Zyl – could see something in her that would make her a good forward. She excelled as a hooker, being named as Leinster's player of the season the year she received her Ireland call-up. Her subsequent move to the back row was due to a neck injury caused by a disc problem that required surgery. Initially it was thought that Fitzpatrick would never play rugby again, but 'luckily enough, I went to see a really good consultant and things weren't as bad as they thought. I was out of the game for about 18 months, on and off, and managed to work my way back with a lot of physio and a lot of setbacks along the way.' She missed the 2013 grand slam campaign, but shows a philosophical nature in how she coped: 'Any athlete, if you take away playing, that is what you live for, so it was a tough time. But everyone goes through injuries; it is just part and parcel of it. After I went through all that, I missed the 2013 season. It could have been so much worse, not being able to play again. After that, the spine surgeon was saying, "Look, you can't play hooker again" ... I had to go back row at Leinster ... the surgeon and physio ... said "You are not going to survive much longer playing, if you continue playing hooker."'

While she was recovering from her injury, Fitzpatrick was completing her PhD. 'I couldn't run for a long time so even getting back running was quite an achievement. I'm not sure if it was better or worse. I was finishing my PhD at the time of the injury. I was holed up with a laptop, writing non-stop.' That sounds like a rather stressful combination? 'In one way it was nearly a good thing for the PhD because it meant I had so much time to focus on just writing that. Mentally, it was very dark. What really helped me was the Leinster-based Irish girls were training in the gym. I used to go down and do my rehab with them and the team. A lot of times it was depressing. It definitely helped. Spending all day on your own at a computer, not seeing anyone else is not a healthy way to be. Definitely going to see them twice a week and going to do rehab, I would have been very focused on it. This was the best chance I had of getting back.' With her scientific and medical academic background, she decided to learn as much as she could about the type of injury she was suffering from, but as well as being enlightening it could be frightening to know in such detail what her body was going though: 'I ended up doing a load of research into neck injuries. I taught myself to read MRI imaging as well. I had been given the disc of my scan but the doctor wasn't going to give me the report for a week. So I learnt a lot about it. In some cases it was a bad thing to know so much information because it was a lot of the catastrophe situations, but I ended up reading and writing a load on it and looking at one stage to apply for funding to do a study on neck injuries. I was very much consumed by it.'

It is interesting that as Fitzpatrick talks me through this Six Nations campaign she barely mentions some of the victories, instead speaking in detail about the loss against France and admitting that it dominates her thoughts: 'I still think about that loss. I'd think about it more than the games I've won. The French are such huge rivals of us, particularly as a back row. Playing against their back row is a big motivational factor for us. It is probably the same for all the positions. The French are one of the best teams in the world, and the grand slam year we managed to beat them. We've never beaten France away from home. It is quite a big thing ... because we had the opportunity to do it, because it was within our grasp. Devastating. Really, really devastating.' This shows Fitzpatrick's competitive streak and reveals some of the desire that helped her return to the Irish set-up from a serious injury, while also shifting position, to become an integral part of the 2014 World Cup squad.

You also get the impression that part of the reason she enjoys being on the Irish team is that she was at one point so close to having to give up on rugby. The enthusiasm with which she describes the build-up to a match again shows how much she relishes the competition and the camaraderie: 'It is very much a team thing, feeling connected to the team and connecting with people. I love that. We have meals the morning of the games and it's great to have the chats, shoot the breeze and slag each other.

'Some matches are different. You need to be in your own space and focus on what you need to do. We always have our music in the changing room and that is when the back row comes in: we have our shoulder shimmy dance!' On the topic of her back-row colleagues: 'Heather and Molloy are the hardest workers and they just go looking for work. I wouldn't want to play beside anyone else. They are legends. We would all be really good friends and we have our little ritual before games. We would always have a group hug and say what we want to do. Our mission is to beat our opposite number and then beat the opposition back row.' The evening before the Wales match, news came from Badia Polesine in northern Italy that the Azzurre had earned a famous victory against France, derailing Les Bleues' grand slam ambitions and opening the door for Ireland to go into the final round of competition level on points with the French. They would have a very realistic shot at claiming the Six Nations, but only if they could beat the Welsh.

As a result: 'We were very focused on just getting the win. Historically, Wales has been a very tough place to go. We have generally not won that many times in Wales. We were expecting it to be a close match.' Head coach Tom Tierney made one change to the team that had overcome England 11–8 in Ashbourne in the previous round. Katie Fitzhenry was ruled out due to an ankle injury she picked up in training. Jackie Shiels was named at inside centre, with Aoife Doyle taking her spot on the replacements bench. It was also a special day for hooker Gillian Bourke, as she joined the 50 caps club. Fitzpatrick explains that the match also had special meaning for her back-row colleague Molloy, who practises medicine in Cardiff: 'With Claire and Larissa Muldoon living in Wales ... it brings an extra dynamic to the match for them because they are playing against their club-mates.'

The match was played in the picturesque seaside St Helen's ground in Swansea. Fitzpatrick recalls: 'It was quite tight, quite a physical game to begin with and we were dominating to some extent but we weren't getting the scores on the board. Heather had to go off injured then and Orla Fitzsimons had to come on ... so Sophie Spence moved into the back row and Orla went in the second row. I moved to eight and she is six, it is a bit of a disruption but Sophie did a great job ... and so did Orla in the second row; I think she wouldn't have had much game time before that, I think she really did well. At the time when she came on ... we were defending quite vigorously and there were quite a few tackles to be put in.'

What Fitzpatrick fails to mention is that she scored the match's opening try with 27 minutes on the clock: this and Niamh Briggs' conversion were the only points of the first half. It seems that she would rather heap the praise on her teammates: 'One of the most outstanding things of that game was Claire Molloy ... I think she stole ... four or five balls at the breakdown, which Briggsy was able to kick over. It is like Molloy just needs to be unleashed. What she is really good at doing is stealing the ball off the deck. Exactly like David Pocock – even better, I'd say! She owns the breakdown.' Fitzpatrick felt that the 20–nil final score flattered

Ireland, 'because Ali Miller got a try at the end but it felt like quite a tight game for the duration. To get those penalties, was really, really important.'

It was a case of 'game on' as Ireland headed into their encounter with the Scots the following week. As Fitzpatrick says, 'Italy had beaten France, so that was huge news for us ... because we were depending on the other results after the loss to France.' The Irish and French were the only sides to have won three of their four fixtures. After injury had so cruelly denied her in 2013, could this be Paula Fitzpatrick's opportunity to be part of a Six Nations winning side?

WALES 0, IRELAND 20
ST HELEN'S, SWANSEA,
14 MARCH 2015

Wales: D Hywel (K Lake 52); L Harries, A Taviner, G Rowland, E Evans; E Snowsill (H Jones 80), A Day (K Bevan 80); J Davies (C Thomas 52), C Phillips (A Lawrence 77), C Edwards (A Evans 60); J Hawkins (R Rowe 77), R Taylor (capt); S Williams (M Clay 80), S Harries, S Powell Hughes.

Ireland: N Briggs (capt); H Tyrrell (A Doyle 80+5), J Murphy, J Shiels (S Naoupu 20–26), A Miller; N Stapleton (Naoupu 68), L Muldoon (Rosser 55); R O'Reilly (F Hayes 55), G Bourke (S Mimnagh 80+5), A Egan (F O'Brien 80+5); S Spence (K Norris 80+5), ML Reilly; P Fitzpatrick, C Molloy, H O'Brien (O Fitzsimons 34).

Referee: C Hodnett (England).

Scoring sequence: 27 mins: Fitzpatrick try, Briggs conv 0–7; 48 mins: Briggs pen 0–10; 61 mins: Briggs pen 0–13; 80 mins: Miller try, Briggs conv 0–20.

12

WALES:
JOHNNY SEXTON

Peter O'Reilly

A two-week gap between Rounds Three and Four was welcome for Joe Schmidt and especially for his medical and rehab staff, but it left a lot of space to be filled for daily newspaper reporters. In situations like this, Wales coach Warren Gatland can be a saviour of sorts. He can usually be relied upon to take the odd pot-shot during the course of a Six Nations campaign, and if Ireland is the opponent, he can be especially trigger-happy – it may be something to do with the fact that he coached them for three and a half seasons around the turn of the millennium. A few weeks previously, his defence coach Shaun Edwards had ruffled feathers by calling for the choke tackle – patented by Les Kiss – to be outlawed. What next? Perhaps a barbed comment about Ireland's reliance on kick-chase? Maybe something on Johnny Sexton's fractious relationship with certain Welsh Lions? But Gatland and Edwards were ominously respectful towards their opponents. Having seen their team beaten 3–26 in Dublin the previous season, it wasn't like they had much option.

The Irish media had to move on to other matters – like Paul O'Connell, and the fact that he was about to become the fourth Irish player to reach a century of international caps, and how his partnership with Schmidt was maturing. 'The person I have come to know is exactly the person I thought he was from afar,' said Schmidt. 'He has got incredible self-drive, and he's an incredibly intelligent man about the game, and about particular aspects of the game. He is incredibly driven to improve his own performance and thereby leads others in doing that.'

The media focused on how Ireland were closing in on a record 11th consecutive victory and, of course, they wrote about the possibility of a grand slam. People drew comparisons with 2009. The schedule was not dissimilar to that campaign, culminating with games in Edinburgh and Cardiff (though not in that order). Ireland's selection profile was similar also. The impressive work of Ian Keatley, Jordi Murphy and Tommy O'Donnell created the impression of depth but, in fact, Schmidt had only 18 starters thus far and was unlikely to indulge in any experimentation for the Millennium Stadium. As the roadshow moved to Belfast for a two-day camp, we learned that Sean O'Brien and Jared Payne were recovering well from their respective concussions against England and were looking good to start against Wales. Jamie Heaslip's back was also coming along nicely and he was likely to be the only change in the starting line-up – on the assumption that Sexton's hamstring recovered in time.

The promising bit was that Sexton was there in Belfast, albeit only in an autograph-signing capacity. Racing Métro had already decided he had no chance of being fit to play Grenoble the Saturday before Cardiff, so he could spend as much time as possible with Schmidt's battery of physios and masseurs. Ireland's dependency on their out-half was underlined further when Brian O'Driscoll was heard to pronounce on national radio that Sexton was now not merely the best number 10 in the world but 'probably the best rugby player in the world too'. And so, even the official press release carried a tone of relief when the announcement came, the following Tuesday, that Sexton would be ready for the Millennium, even if his participation in training would be limited.

This was a special game for Sexton – his 50th cap for his country, against a country with which he has a special relationship. Three of the Welsh players – Dan Lydiate, Jamie Roberts and Luke Charteris – had been club-mates of his at Racing, while he had played in the same Lions Test team as Lydiate, Roberts, Jonathan Davies, George North, Leigh Halfpenny, Alun-Wyn Jones, Sam Warburton and Taulupe Faletau. In his book *Becoming a Lion*, Sexton had described what it was like to win a Test series in a team coached by Gatland, with 10 Welshmen in the starting line-up, and how, after winning, he had jokingly led a rendition of 'Bread of Heaven' on the team bus. He liked the Millennium Stadium too. 'An incredible stadium – I think it rates right up there for most of us,' Sexton says. 'I've had mixed experiences there. I lost there with Ireland in 2011, when I missed an important penalty, but a couple of months later, Leinster had that amazing comeback against Northampton in the final of the Heineken Cup. I'd won there with Ireland in 2013 also, when we had a 20–0 lead but ended up having to fight for our lives as Wales came back at us.'

This game had a markedly different pattern, with Wales exploding out of the blocks to build a 12–0 lead at the rate of a point a minute. It was a dizzying experience, even just sitting in the press box. The media's working conditions at the Millennium are far from ideal – pitch-side seats, virtually at worm's-eye level, mean that when the action is on the far side of the playing surface, your view is so restricted that you're better off following the play on one of the giant screens at either end of the arena. At the same time, being so close to the pitch means you get a much more vivid sense of how gladiatorial these contests are, how frenzied the pace, how seismic every thud. The celestial light that floods the pitch when the roof is open only adds to the drama. That day, Wales were suitably inspired.

Notoriously slow starters to the tournament, Gatland's men had paid for a weak half an hour against England, and were then probably a little fortunate to escape from Murrayfield with a win. They'd hit their straps in Paris, however, and now looked thoroughly prepared for Ireland's bombing campaign. When Sexton or Conor Murray kicked up the middle,

Halfpenny rose majestically and made every ball his. Wales chased their own kicks feverishly, too, but were also willing to run and handle, with Davies looking particularly sharp. On one bullocking run up the left flank, he flattened Sexton with a lethal fend.

The force was with Wales, and so too was the referee. It's rare that a referee will officiate the same team twice in the course of a championship, but when Steve Walsh cried off for this fixture for 'business reasons', Wayne Barnes was given the gig – his second game involving Ireland in the space of a month. At times, it looked like a case of his familiarity with them breeding contempt – 'Be quiet!' he said, in his most peremptory tone, when Sean O'Brien queried one decision at the ruck. Barnes crucified Ireland at the ruck before the break and even gave them a hard time at the scrum – despite the fact that the visitors were clearly dominant in this phase, especially after Wales had lost tight-head prop Samson Lee to injury after 12 minutes. (They would also lose Gethin Jenkins, their veteran loose-head, at half-time.)

The upshot of Wales's dynamic opening was that Ireland were in the rare situation of having to chase a game. But how to chase? Having seen Wales take ownership of the air, and how they were consistently keeping two men in the backfield, Sexton realised that the only space to kick into was just behind the red defensive wall, and that was a ploy that could only work once or twice. He felt compelled to keep the ball in hand more, to try a few planned moves a channel or two from the ruck. But Ireland's execution wasn't always what it could have been – hardly surprising, given that they were effectively trying a game they hadn't yet played that season. His own execution was a little rusty, too – probably the effect of having trained properly only once that week. One restart flew a metre too far and went out on the full. The same happened with a left-footed punt. Had he been rattled by that Davies fend early on?

'No, I was just off-balance and he pushed me on my arse!' says Sexton. 'It wasn't a good moment for me but I wasn't rattled. We just made too many mistakes, especially in the first half. We'd spoken about discipline but then we started by conceding lots of penalties, whether rightly or wrongly. Then we made errors that we hadn't been making in the championship up to that point. I kicked a couple of balls that went out on the full – a yard shorter and they'd have been decent kicks. We had miscommunications. One time I was trying to organise the next phase and Jamie thought I was calling for the ball so I wasn't ready for it when it came. I don't know if it was the noise of the Millennium or a bit of rustiness – neither of us was as well prepared as we'd have liked. But I was glad with the way we bounced back. This was the first time in the tournament that we had to chase a game. Everything went wrong for us in the first 10–15 minutes but we regrouped and got ourselves back into the game. To get back to 9–15 at the break was a decent effort, I thought.'

As tends to be the case with sides coached by Schmidt, Ireland emerged from the break with renewed purpose and a fresh, almost manic energy. How the third quarter passed without them registering another point remains something of a mystery – or a tribute to the energy and commitment of Wales's defensive effort. By any standards, it was a remarkable performance. Wales smashed the previous tackle-count high of 202, set by Italy, with a final tally of 289. Charteris made a barely credible 37 of those, Warburton 30 – despite spending 10 minutes in the bin. He may have been fortunate to finish the game, seeing as he was the chief culprit when Wales pulled down the Irish maul to concede a penalty try in the final quarter, but then Barnes seemed to apply different standards after the break from before it. When Ireland went through multiple phases in possession during the third quarter, they felt the referee was more lenient when Welsh players were slow to roll away from the tackle. That said, the visitors' decision-making and execution in that period was panicky.

'We felt we should have been awarded more penalties when we were dominating possession, but they're the breaks when you're playing away from home,' says Sexton. 'Wales did what they had to do and I remember the enormous roar from their supporters when one of those attacks ended with me being penalised for going off my feet at the ruck. It was poor execution from me and of course, Joe picked it up at the video review! In fairness to Wales, it was a big moment and I'm sure it gave them a huge lift. They'd withstood massive pressure and that was probably the winning of the game. We'd worked so hard for nothing in return and then Wales went down our end and scored a try [by Scott Williams] where they didn't seem to have to work hard at all.'

Williams's try came courtesy of a couple of Irish errors – a lineout malfunction in their own 22, then a rare defensive error by Heaslip.

Halfpenny missed the conversion but the Wales lead stood at 20–9 with 19 minutes remaining. Cue mass substitutions on both sides, with Ireland's bench having the more positive impact. The penalty try reduced the gap to four points before Halfpenny virtually guaranteed Wales at least a share of the points when he kicked his fifth penalty of the afternoon with only five minutes on the clock. That still allowed Ireland time to make one final surge. With just five seconds on the clock, Wales had a put-in five metres from their own line. Barnes saw Mike Phillips feed the ball crooked, saw the Welsh scrum run backwards yet somehow awarded them a penalty, apparently against Cian Healy, apparently on the say-so of his assistant referee, Federico Anselmi. 'I'm still at a loss as to what it was for,' says Mike Ross. Still, how appropriate that the game should end thus – with a penalty against Ireland.

Reactions to the game differed wildly. Former Welsh internationals proclaimed it a majestic affair, made marvellous by Wales's heroism in defence. Certainly Warburton and co. *were* heroic, but if long periods of red shirts tackling one-out runners in green shirts is your idea of thrilling rugby, so be it. On the one hand, you felt Ireland deserved to lose given that their attacking limitations had been exposed; on the other, it felt like the referee had been far too influential. For the second time in a month, the number of penalties conceded by Ireland had soared into double figures – 11 was significantly higher than their norm. Irish supporters detected a trend when it came to Wayne Barnes and matches involving these two countries. When Ireland had scraped their grand slam win six years previously, he had penalised them 15 times to six decisions against the Welsh. In 2012, there had been that hotly disputed and match-turning red card against Stephen Ferris. He'd also been the ref when Wales won 16–12 in Croke Park in 2008.

Schmidt chose not to make the ref the story, however. 'There's got to be some credit to the Welsh,' he said. 'They're never going to make it easy here. After a defeat like this, I struggle to sleep. I think about the what-ifs and maybes because there were a fair few. These results come down to narrow margins. But we have to take a look at ourselves. We weren't good enough today but at the same time, what I don't want is that we suddenly lose our confidence. We've just got to rub a little bit out and add a little bit here and there, and try to construct something that works in Murrayfield.'

He also needed to find a way of putting a smile back on the face of his play-maker. Sexton always struggles to sleep the night of a game and after a loss, he finds himself replaying each critical moment, as if attempting to rewrite the scene. He didn't need to be told the consequences of defeat. England were now top of the Six Nations table, level with Ireland and Wales on six match points but four points ahead on overall points differential at +37 – a crucial advantage, especially as their game against France would be the last of the tournament – unlike other competitions, the Six Nations staggers kick-offs across its final day. Ireland, with a points differential of +33, were on second in Murrayfield, after Wales attempted to improve their differential of +12 in Rome. The bookies made England 8/11 favourites, with Ireland now 6/4 to retain the title and Wales outsiders at 9/1.

'That was our chance gone to win a Slam,' says Sexton, 'and that made the day hugely disappointing, one of the worst. At that point I reckoned the championship was gone, too. I knew Wales would have a crack in Rome but it was all set up for England.'

WALES 23, IRELAND 16
MILLENNIUM STADIUM, 14 MARCH 2015

Wales: L Halfpenny; G North, J Davies, J Roberts (S Williams 60), L Williams; D Biggar, R Webb (M Phillips 69); G Jenkins (R Evans h-t), S Baldwin (R Hibbard 57), S Lee (A Jarvis 15); L Charteris, A-W Jones (J Ball 72); D Lydiate (J Tipuric 69), S Warburton (capt), T Faletau.
Sin-binned: Warburton (27–37 mins), Davies (78 mins).

Ireland: R Kearney; T Bowe, J Payne, R Henshaw, S Zebo; J Sexton (I Madigan 75), C Murray (E Reddan 63); J McGrath (C Healy 57), R Best (S Cronin 63), M Ross (M Moore 63); D Toner (I Henderson 63), P O'Connell (capt); P O'Mahony, S O'Brien, J Heaslip (J Murphy 72).

Referee: Wayne Barnes (England).

Scoring sequence: 2 mins: Halfpenny pen 3–0; 7 mins: Halfpenny pen 6–0; 11 mins: Halfpenny pen 9–0; 14 mins: Halfpenny pen 12–0; 18 mins: Sexton pen 12–3; 30 mins: Sexton pen 12–6; 34 mins: Biggar drop-goal 15–6; 37 mins: Sexton pen 15–9; 62 mins: S Williams try 20–9; 69 mins: penalty try, Sexton con 20–16; 75 mins: Halfpenny pen 23–16.

13

SCOTLAND: NIAMH BRIGGS

Kate Rowan

Niamh Briggs is the embodiment of the fabled old-fashioned Munster rugby spirit. Ireland's women's captain and full-back both plays and speaks with her heart on her sleeve, honestly detailing how she becomes racked with anxiety before every match. Yet it would seem that a steely determination to fight alongside her teammates causes these nerves to disappear the moment she takes to the field.

One of the catalysts in creating a whole new generation of rugby fans in Ireland from the late nineties and early noughties was how, during Munster's halcyon Heineken Cup days, people could emotionally connect and empathise with that combination of raw emotion, doggedness, underdog mentality and stoicism, all stitched together with a strong thread of humility. Even if they were not fully acquainted with the finer technical nuances of the game or they had not grown up surrounded by a rugby culture, fans of all ages and provinces hopped on the Munster bandwagon.

Of course the legendary pride and passion that helped to fuel the bandwagon, and propelled sayings such as 'Superman wears Paul O'Connell pyjamas' into popular parlance, came from a heritage rooted in the amateur era. The almost mythical victory against the All Blacks in 1978 contributed to building what would become the Munster brand of the professional era.

Briggs can also claim to be part of an exclusive club of All Black – or, more properly, Black Fern – slayers after Ireland's landmark victory over New Zealand in the Women's Rugby World Cup in 2014. However, following in the tradition of Munster's amateur and professional men, Briggs comes across as deeply self-deprecating and possesses an extremely likeable and relatable 'girl next door' quality.

The contrast between Briggs becoming choked up during the anthems and how resolute she appears in striving for success on the field again brings to mind her male Munster and Ireland counterparts such as Peter O'Mahony. However, the key difference is that the men are professionals, while the women as amateurs must juggle playing for club, province and country with careers outside rugby.

Ireland's final fixture of the 2015 Six Nations campaign, against Scotland, was the culmination of a period of intense juggling of rugby, work and personal lives for each squad member. Head coach Tom Tierney named a side unchanged from the one that had put Wales to the sword the previous week. The team would have the opportunity to seize history after the grand-slam-hunting French had capitulated against the Italians in the previous round.

The occasion was obviously a landmark for each woman in green, but it held an extra significance for Captain Briggs, as the match in Broadwood Stadium, Cumbernauld – a satellite town to Glasgow – would mark her 50th cap. Being 'crippled with fear' on the eve of the match was part of the process Briggs endures before every international: 'I am a very emotional type of person, so I would normally cry before each match, during the anthems and that. This year I was trying to fix that because I am trying to work on the positive side. I didn't allow myself to get as emotional that night before but I was still getting sick at five o'clock in the morning.' This sort of nerves is indicative of an individual who is giving every inch of herself for the cause. In order to understand what motivated the Ireland captain to this extent, it is important to travel back a few years with Niamh Briggs.

The other part of her life – as a member of An Garda Síochána based in Limerick City, working as a community garda in areas with 'tough' reputations, such as Southill – helps to shed further light on her character. To a journalist listening to Briggs the rugby player and Ireland captain during this Six Nations campaign she always came across as confident and self-assured. However, she points out that this was not always the case, and credits her work in policing: 'When I first joined the Guards, I probably would not have been the most confident person. It has taught me how to be assertive, to respect people and to probably understand people without jumping the gun, to take a minute to assess the situation. That has helped me massively on a rugby pitch ... when things are all gung-ho and [you] just need to be able to clear your mind for a second. The Guards has probably contributed a massive amount to my rugby and probably vice versa, my rugby has contributed massively to my role in the Guards. So, they complement each other very well.'

Briggs, now 30, commenced her Garda training in 2008 – the year she made her test match debut for Ireland against Italy in the Six Nations. She would spend Monday to Friday attending to her policing studies in Templemore, and at the weekend there was little rest as she travelled to Dublin to train with the national squad.

It is with terrific warmth that Briggs describes working with young-sters as part of her remit in community policing: 'There is a group of kids from the regeneration areas in Limerick – Southill and Ballinacurra Weston – I take them out on Tuesdays and Thursdays to do soccer and rugby at Garryowen Rugby Club. They get their dinner there. It is a fan-tastic way for me to get a foothold into that area; I came down and I knew nobody and they didn't know who I was, so it was a good way for the kids to be able to see me without the uniform on, building up a relationship with them. It has been fantastic, now they know me and I know them. It is not from a crime point of view; it never was that, it was about building up that trust. It gets the kids out, to be physically active and that in turn helps their mental state. It can only be a positive for them.'

An Garda Síochána and rugby, however, were not always the cornerstones of Briggs' life. Much of her childhood was spent moving around Ireland due to her father Mike's job in the digital and later pharma industries, yet there was one constant in her youth: sport. She recalls that 'I was incredibly sporty as a child; my mother had difficulty keeping me in the house! When I was younger, having moved around so much, it was probably a connection for me to make with other people. I would have played any kind of sport that was going and you learn to make friends from that.' The family settled for good in Dungarvan, which is very much home for Niamh and her two elder brothers Shane and Liam and younger sister Roisin.

Like many of her Ireland colleagues, Briggs did not start to play rugby until she was in third-level education, doing exercise and health studies in the Waterford Institute of Technology. Prior to that Gaelic football had become her main focus: she played all the way up to senior inter-county level, winning various under-age All-Ireland titles. Her ultimate ambition was 'to play in Croke Park – I wanted to lift a trophy, I wanted to lift the Brendan Martin Cup for Waterford, that was my aspiration.'

Briggs' conversion to the oval ball was something of an epiphany: 'I had been playing football for a long time and it was not like I fell out of love with it but I had been knocked back a couple of times by different coaches. When I got to rugby, it was the type of game that suited me and there was great camaraderie straight away with all the girls I played with, there was a great team spirit – not that there wasn't that with football. It was just there was something different about it in rugby and that appealed to me. Without sounding arrogant, I was naturally much better at rugby than I was at football. I felt like I had to work very hard just to be able to play football. Playing rugby just seemed a lot easier for me. Maybe it was because I wasn't incredibly fit endurance-wise but I had great power, and rugby was much more powerful whereas football was more about endurance.'

The honesty comes to the fore again as Briggs describes her younger self: 'It wasn't that I was overly aggressive but I was extremely competitive when I was younger – too much so – at school, club level at football, and I was probably seen to be a little bit too big for my boots. It wasn't that I was cheeky or aggressive, it was the fact that I was so competitive that I *really, really* wanted to win. When I lost, I took it very, very badly. Rugby seemed to help that.'

That will to win, although perhaps tempered, is still very apparent in the successes Briggs has achieved over the past seven or eight seasons, but she rarely gives herself much credit. It is with great fondness, affection and deference that she describes her rugby mentors and friends: initially at club level for Clonmel, where her dad coached her on the women's team, and then at UL Bohemians, where some of the pioneers of the women's game such as Fiona Steed and Fiona Coghlan were key influences. Current Munster men's defence and kicking coach Ian Costello was another who helped to shape her game. Despite being a prominent member of Ireland's grand-slam-winning side of 2013, she seems more comfortable talking about the fight she had in breaking through to become a fixture at international level in 2008, and name-checks former backline colleagues Sarahjane Belton and Lynne Cantwell as well as Tania Rosser, who was part of this season's Six Nations squad: 'amazing players – I had to earn it'.

Fast-forward to early 2015: Briggs is now a leading light of the Irish backline after the 2013 grand slam season and of course her string of virtuoso performances during Ireland's run to the 2014 World Cup semi-finals, leading to her being named in the team of the tournament and shortlisted for the IRB Women's Player of the Year award. With the retirements of captain Coghlan and key leader Cantwell, now was the time for new leaders to step up. For the previous few seasons Briggs had assumed a leadership role in the backs: as she explains, 'I always enjoyed it but Fi and Lynne would have always been there to fall back on. You would always depend on them if something wasn't going right.' Receiving the captaincy was something of a surprise for her: 'I definitely wasn't expecting it. I was injured going into Six Nations. It wasn't even in my head; I was just trying to get back to fitness. It wasn't that I wouldn't have seen myself as captain material but it was definitely a bit of a shock. I quickly had to get myself in order. Fiona Coghlan was an amazing captain, she was incredibly good at speaking and it was an aspect or area I felt I had to work on, but I knew if I could play well, and lead on the pitch, at least I was doing the girls some sort of service. It was a tremendous honour but a bit weird because you are so used to hearing someone else speaking in a huddle before a match. Then everyone stops and looks at you, so it is a bit daunting.'

Briggs did not have to stray far from home to obtain advice about leading a team: her elder brother Shane had until this season been captain of Waterford's inter-county senior football side. 'Shane has been a massive influence on me, in terms of he has been there, done that. Especially this year with me being made captain, he was able to give me plenty of sound advice. Obviously before the Italy game, it was my first as captain, so I was a bit nervous. So, I rang him up the morning of the match and I was like, "what am I going to say?" He talked to me to try to calm me down before I freaked out! He gave me a couple of pointers. He spoke to me really, really well. I was fine and I was able to hold myself together. His influence on me was massive for it.'

The sense of honesty surrounding her personal development is again brought into focus: 'As the years have gone on, I have come out of my shell a little bit. I would have always been fairly vocal on the pitch but off it, not so much. This year was a little bit harder in that sense but I learnt a lot. I sought advice where I could. I spoke to some of the professional lads about leadership.' These mentors included Ireland's men's captain Paul O'Connell and Munster full-back Felix Jones, who has often assumed captaincy duties. 'The Munster boys are great sounding boards. You are constantly striving to be better; you are constantly looking for better ways to communicate with people. I am learning all the time. I don't want to stop learning.' However, she is keen to emphasise that 'It is important I fit it into my own style because you don't want to be replicating something, because it doesn't mean anything then.' Briggs credits her teammates with helping to smooth the transition into her new role: 'In fairness to the squad, it wasn't that much different to other years, bar for the toss at the start of the match – I didn't really have to do much else because the girls stood up and took a lot of responsibility. We have a lot of experience in that squad and they were excellent.'

The affection and admiration in which Briggs holds her fellow players is apparent as, with a huge smile, she describes her side's journeys to matches on the team coach this season: 'I know that Maz [Marie Louise Reilly], Jenny [Murphy] and Nora [Stapleton] will sit on the back of the bus on the way to a match and will make jokes: the stupidest jokes you will ever hear. I know that [Sophie] Spence and Gillian [Bourke] will sit in the middle of the bus, listening to their music and will concentrate on the match. I know that Paula Fitzpatrick, Heather O'Brien, Ruth O'Reilly, Orla Fitzsimons, that group will have random sing-songs, burst out into random songs.' And what about the captain herself? 'I am the one who sits in the middle of the bus. For years Grace Davitt was my bus buddy, we would sit opposite Joy Neville and Fiona Coghlan, then they retired, so this year it was Katie Norris.' With a wry chuckle she continues: 'She has good luck to sit beside me on the bus! We usually just chat or listen to music. I am usually incredibly nervous before matches. I would be up to 90 before most matches. Katie is good because she is a calming influence; so was Grace.'

Another glimpse into the team dynamic is given as Briggs reveals that 'I very much just like to sit back, watch the girls and laugh at them. But for me the most important thing is that there are no cliques. It is the fact that everybody brings something different. That is really important because if we were all clones we could all win but we would never enjoy it. Or you would rock up to training and you would be dreading the weekend in camp, whereas we don't. We love the fact that we spend time together and we get on well. We work incredibly hard on the pitch but are also incredibly giddy off it.'

With much laughter, some of the sources of the giddiness are explained, starting with the front row players – or 'fromance', as they are known: 'They are very clannish, it is very hard to get in there! Great for bringing treats to each other but don't bring them around to the rest of us! Then the back row girls have their own little dancing thing going on, a shoulder shimmy thing that they do! You can't be a bit sensitive, everybody takes the piss back.' The serious, focused side returns as Briggs clarifies that 'the most important thing is that it works for us; it might not work for anybody else but it works for us. Anybody who has come into the squad, particularly this year, have adapted really well to it, which is great.'

So, back to the evening of Saturday, 21 March 2015. As Ireland's men got word that they could finally celebrate a Six Nations triumph in Edinburgh, Niamh Briggs was feeling 'the most nervous I have ever been. I was getting sick and I think I only had two hours' sleep. Up until then, we hadn't been expected to win that many of the games. When you go into a game where you are expected to win, it heaps another load of pressure on you.' Ireland's women were probably some of the very few members of the Irish rugby community who had missed out on watching their male counterparts beat the Scots at Murrayfield: 'we didn't watch the men's game as we had our Captain's Run. For the England's men's game Jenny Murphy and myself had gone to the stadium to do our kicking. When we arrived at the stadium, Jenny was trying to refresh her phone and we found out the men had won ... So, we had a little "woo-hoo!" celebration, just me, Jenny, Jean [Casey] our manager and Lukasz our strength and conditioner. When we got back to our hotel, the women's England versus France match was on. I watched it for a couple of minutes and I realised "I cannot watch this"; I went back to my room and I pottered about; I did anything but watch rugby or think about rugby. We had a team meeting scheduled, so I got back up in time to watch the end of the match. England had scored a try in the 78th minute to bring it back to 27 points: I knew at the time 27 was achievable whereas before it was 33 and I thought 33 might be a bit much for us. I don't think I ever celebrated an English try so much! I jumped down from my seat and I was jumping around the place!'

Then came that almost sleepless night.

On match day there was the comforting routine of the bus journey, the calming influence of her 'bus buddy' Norris, then arriving at the stadium to see that 'My dad was there, Fi [Coghlan] and Lynne [Cantwell] were there, it was fine. Then we got out onto the pitch: for our warm-up there was a big breeze and it was hard to kick.' Briggs, with the responsibility of being her side's designated kicker, was acutely aware that in order to bridge the points difference to clinch the Championship, she might need to be near metronomic with her boot.

Yet again, Briggs' honest and self-critical nature comes to the fore as she tells how her kicking technique has progressed: 'Up until last year, anything would have gone through my mind and I found it very hard to focus. I found it very hard to block everything out around me. Maybe in the last nine, 12 months it is something I have worked very hard on.' Throughout this campaign she implemented a routine to aid this psychological aspect of placekicking: 'I have four words in my head – I am not going to tell you what they are. I say those four words over and over to block out what is around me; it allows me to concentrate on the process of kicking the ball over the bar.' That constant desire to improve and humility again show as she points out some of her weaker performances at the kicking tee: 'I have had good and bad days. The Italy match was incredibly hard for me. You miss five or six and you almost don't know what is going wrong because you think what you are doing is right and then obviously it is not, so that can be very hard.'

Improvement for the subsequent matches came in the form of rigorous practice: kicking every day for a minimum of 30 to 45 minutes in order to get herself 'into a good enough confident rhythm'. This extra kicking practice was slotted in around Briggs' busy work schedule. She also received expert tuition from Dave Alred, famed for his work with

Jonny Wilkinson, because 'Adidas sponsor my boots and stuff. He was over helping Johnny [Sexton] and I was invited in. We did very little kicking; we just spoke a lot about the mental side of it.' This shows how far Briggs has risen in the game, considering that when she first took up the sport she would spend hours watching YouTube videos of Wilkinson and Ronan O'Gara to teach herself kicking technique. Briggs also credits Ian Costello with helping to improve her kicking form throughout the tournament: 'Speaking to Cossie and Dave, they emphasised how important it is that you keep plugging away and thinking about the process of what you are doing and the end product will eventually come.'

Finally it was the moment of truth. Could Ireland beat Scotland by 27 points to take home the Women's Six Nations? Could they withstand the pressure as favourites to help make 2015 the first ever season that both the Irish men and women would be anointed as the best in northern hemisphere rugby?

A few months on, the excitement is still audible in Briggs' voice: 'To lead out the girls for a match like that was probably the proudest moment of my life. It is your 50th cap and you are there for your anthem in a potential championship-winning match – it was amazing.'

When retelling the story of the match, Briggs fails to mention that she scored the opening try after just four minutes: 'To get off to a really good start, we got the first try, then Claire Molloy got the second try and … I looked at Jenny and I said, "We are going to win this!"' This summation says it all about the Ireland women's class of 2015: the 'we' always comes before 'I'. And then there was the self-belief of champions, which helped Ireland to run riot against the Scots.

Classy Irish play blitzed an abject Scottish defence, with wing Alison Miller scoring a hat-trick. After Briggs' and Molloy's opening salvos, tries in the first half came from number eight Heather O'Brien, hooker Bourke and Miller. This took the half-time score to 3–37. Unhappily, wing Hannah Tyrrell, after setting up Briggs' opening try, dislocated her shoulder and spent the afternoon in hospital.

Ireland began the second half at breakneck pace, with Miller scoring her second try after just two minutes. Blindside Fitzpatrick then scored, followed by the explosive second row Spence scoring the last of the forwards' tries. Replacement scrum half Rosser, Miller and outside centre Murphy all scored tries in the final three minutes of play.

With her try, penalties and conversions, Briggs contributed 23 points to the 73–3 scoreline. Naturally, though, that was another detail she omitted from her reporting of that glorious afternoon in Broadwood Stadium. What she has to say is much more poignant and significant for what that match meant, means and will mean for Irish women's rugby: 'I loved the fact that we went to another level – it was the most satisfying thing that we absolutely became ruthless. We have never been able to do that in all the years I have been playing for Ireland. We had always been considered too nice, so to keep turning the screw like we did was amazing. It was surreal after about 60 minutes to look at the clock and know you have won a Championship, you are playing on this artificial soccer pitch, the stand is full of Irish people and you know your mother is at home watching it. It was unreal!'

Unfortunately, the day was not entirely perfect for Briggs: 'I had gotten really badly injured in the first half – I was trying to talk myself through the second half, so that was an incredible high afterwards. But then the knee injury brings you back down to a massive low. I wasn't able to enjoy it as much. The final whistle goes and you don't know whether to laugh or to cry. Then it all hits you – you look across at the scoreboard … you look at 70-odd points and you look across at the Scottish girls and you can't help but feel a little bit sorry for them.'

Despite the pain, 'I ran straight over to my dad and I celebrated with the girls. I did something I didn't think I would ever do – to lift the trophy after such an amazing performance, to be a 50-cap captain. It was probably the best day of my life, in terms of my rugby career.'

SCOTLAND 3, IRELAND 73
BROADWOOD STADIUM,
22 MARCH 2015

Scotland: C Rollie (C Bain 71); N Deans, G Inglis, H Smith, E Sinclair; L Martin, S Law (M Greene 55); L Robertson (H Lockhart 51), L Skeldon (L Smith 55), T Balmer (capt); D McCormack, E Wassell; R Cook (L O'Donnell h-t), K Dunbar, J Konkel.

Ireland: N Briggs (capt); H Tyrrell (A Doyle 20), J Murphy, J Shiels

(S Naoupu 57), A Miller; N Stapleton, L Muldoon (T Rosser 57); R O'Reilly (F Hayes 52), G Bourke (S Mimnagh 75), A Egan (F O'Brien 75); S Spence (O Fitzsimons 67), ML Reilly; P Fitzpatrick (K Norris 72), C Molloy, H O'Brien.

Referee: J Beard (New Zealand).

Scoring sequence: 4 mins: Briggs try 0–5; 12 mins: Briggs pen 0–8; 14 mins: Deans pen 3–8; 17 mins: Molloy try 3–13; 25 mins: O'Brien try, Briggs con 3–20; 30 mins: Bourke try, Briggs con 3–27; 36 mins: Briggs pen 3–30; 38 mins: Miller try, Briggs con 3–37; 42 mins: Miller try, Briggs con 3–44; 50 mins: Fitzpatrick try 3–49; 62 mins: Spence try, Briggs con 3–56; 76 mins: Rosser try, Briggs con 3–63; 78 mins: Miller try 3–68; Murphy try 3–73.

14

SCOTLAND: LUKE FITZGERALD

Peter O'Reilly

After the disappointment of Cardiff, Paul O'Connell had spoken of wanting to 'turn the page quickly' and to focus on the challenge of Scotland seven days later. This wasn't as simple as it sounded. His players were beaten up, mentally and physically, and training sessions on Monday and Tuesday felt flat. Joe Schmidt wisely resisted the urge to work his players too hard in the areas where they'd been deficient and tried to keep things upbeat, but the sessions were devoid of any spark. He gave the players Wednesday off, as usual, and sensed that they needed the break more than ever. On Tuesday evening he sent out a group text, urging players to enjoy their day off and to come back on Thursday ready to ramp things up.

England had been installed as the bookies' favourites to win the championship, but Schmidt was still confident Ireland could pull it off. Having looked at the maths, he came up with a number that he thought would help focus minds. That number was 15. If Ireland could beat Scotland by 15 points, Schmidt reckoned they'd win the tournament. But 15 had useful symbolic qualities also. This week had to be about the team, all 15 players. And the performance of those 15 players had to be at least 15 per cent above what it had been at the Millennium Stadium.

Certainly it wouldn't be the same team in terms of personnel. Schmidt revealed two changes when he announced his starting line-up that Thursday afternoon. Cian Healy, who'd been prowling around camp like a caged animal for most of the tournament, would finally be unleashed at the expense of Jack McGrath, while Luke Fitzgerald was to be given a run on the left flank instead of Simon Zebo, who hadn't been nearly as effective against Wales as he'd been against England.

Fitzgerald had been in fine form for Leinster leading up to the tournament and was in the running to be selected for Rome, only to miss the Wolfhounds game. Later in the season, he would give us a fascinating insight into how ravenous top competitors become in this situation and how they cope mentally while waiting for the next opportunity.

'I kind of always felt I'd get a chance and that it was important for me to train really well every day,' Fitzgerald said. 'It's a really hard thing to do but it's what all great teams have: players who aren't picked but who go out to represent the squad and who are all really, really clued in and training hard. You get the news on Tuesday morning – the team is picked and you're not in it – and you've got to go out and train in 15 minutes. So you go from this 'Will I, will I, will I?' situation down to the bottom – 'Ah fuck, I've got to start again.' Excuse my language. But no matter what happened on the Tuesday morning, I was committed in training and working hard. I was seen working hard, being vociferous out there, confident, giving the guys feedback on a move. You don't go into your shell which can happen to you.

'One of my best buddies is sharing a house with me and it's hard for him to comprehend what's happening in here. He's an accountant and his career is 45 years long. Everything in his career is slow and drawn out and patient, whereas in here it's: Boom! One week you're in the team. Next Monday morning, you've had a crap game and Boom! It's back to the start and you've got to go again. It's a really difficult part of the job. You've got to be really process focused to maintain a certain level of performance and to keep getting picked and to stay in the coach's mind.'

And when he finally picks you, do you feel sympathetic towards the guy whose place you've taken?

'I didn't give it a second thought really,' Fitzgerald said. 'Simon's a nice guy and all and you have to be respectful because he's a quality player but I didn't really feel too sorry for the guy who got dropped. It's ruthless and he'd feel the exact same so I don't feel guilty about saying that

I didn't really care about how things were going for him. I was worried about me. And that's all you can do: focus on my own job and then play well at the weekend.'

If this seems hard-nosed, well, it's hardly surprising. Fitzgerald has taken so many knocks in the course of his career that his skin is as thick as a crocodile's. He won his first cap six months after leaving school in 2006, against the Pacific Islanders – the same day that Jamie Heaslip made his Test debut. While Heaslip has 72 caps, a calamitous run of injuries meant that Fitzgerald was making only his 28th appearance in Murrayfield. At 27, he'd won a grand slam and played Test rugby for the Lions yet still hadn't appeared at a Rugby World Cup. The lowest point came in 2012 when he'd undergone neck surgery and found himself out of contract. He hadn't started a Test for Ireland since Bordeaux, August 2011 – Conor Murray's first Test. But here he was, still in the game, still hoping for a break. This was it: a spring day in Edinburgh, when Ireland probably needed to give him the ball.

'Maybe having come straight into professional rugby from school, there was probably a period where I took the job for granted,' Fitzgerald told us. 'But when you've been away for a bit, that hunger and appreciation for it comes back. If you go through hardship, it makes you more appreciative but it also makes you tougher and that's a big advantage I have. When things get tough I always think I'm a little stronger for having gone through the setbacks, for having made the sacrifices.'

Nothing had changed by the time the players arrived in unseasonably warm Edinburgh. A city known for its granite austerity was transformed by sunshine as t-shirted rugby fans sat on the grass and listened to bands outside the stadium. The magic number was still 15, and judging by the half-time score in Rome, Wales had done little to change that – the TV monitors in the tunnel showed that Wales were only a point ahead at 14–13. Italy were apparently lasting the pace well, despite having had one day fewer to prepare than their opponents. The madness would soon begin, however.

The media room for games in Murrayfield is the Bill McLaren 'suite', a narrow, poky room at the back of the stand, just behind that perspex cage where Andy Robinson, the former Scotland coach, used to lose his temper. I'd arrived there around the start of the Italy v Wales game and barely watched the first half, preferring to browse through the Scottish papers, but soon Wales demanded everyone's attention by their brilliance. Italy unravelled in the third quarter, leaking four tries in the space of 12 minutes, including a hat-trick for George North. With 20 minutes remaining, Wales were already ahead of England on points difference and there were further tries for Rhys Webb, Sam Warburton and Scott Williams as they ran the ball from everywhere. Suddenly it looked like 'Super Saturday' might be climaxing a little early. 'Wales move past 60 points and it really does seem that this is going to be too much for England and Ireland to handle,' said BBC's commentator, Alistair Bruce-Ball.

But then in the 77th minute we had the first major turning point of the day, as replacement scrum-half Gareth Davies dropped an intercept pass and thus missed the opportunity to score under the posts – effectively a 14-point swing. Two minutes later, a Welsh defensive lapse allowed Italy's wing, Leonardo Sarto, to score at the other end and Luciano Orquera nailed the conversion. This effectively brought Wales back into range for Ireland and England. Warren Gatland admitted afterwards: 'It was an excellent second-half performance. We thought 50 points would put real pressure on the others but I don't think a difference of 41 points will be enough.'

Ireland had a new target: to win by at least 21 points. Most players remember Schmidt sticking his head into the dressing room huddle to deliver the number, though Sexton only recalls hearing the figure after the anthems, as he prepared to kick off. In retrospect, to have been set a definite target was both a blessing and a spur. Ireland's attack had been blunt so far in the championship – only four tries, compared to 16 the previous season. Now they had a licence to play, and suitable conditions. They didn't wait for a second invitation. With only two minutes on the board, Sexton put Tommy Bowe through a hole in midfield to scatter the Scottish defence and 11 dynamic rucks later, Paul O'Connell was plunging through another hole to score – 7–0 after just five minutes.

It was as if Ireland, Scotland and indeed the whole tournament had been liberated. Suddenly Conor Murray forgot about box-kicking and looked to release his backs. Fitzgerald received more attacking passes in one half than the wings had received all championship. He relished the responsibility, forming a spontaneous relationship with Robbie Henshaw in particular as Ireland explored the wide channels. O'Connell refused to let it become a sevens game, ordering Sexton to kick the points when a penalty opportunity came in the 10th minute. 'Maybe that's why he's the captain,' reflected Sexton subsequently. 'Paulie knew we had to build the win, and knew we had time to rack up the points.' Seven more of those points came courtesy of some deception at the lineout, which saw Devin Toner smuggle the ball to Sean O'Brien, who raced 25 metres to score, looking every inch his old self. Ireland led 17–3 in the 24th minute and looked well on track.

In fairness to the Scots, who were without a win, they were keen to play ball in the sun: especially the young out-half, Finn Russell, who profited from some indecision by Rob Kearney to scamper over for a try. That score, combined with an earlier Russell penalty, convinced O'Connell to continue asking Sexton to kick penalty opportunities, with the result that Ireland went in 20–10 ahead at half-time. Not for the first time, they were inspired by Schmidt's half-time address, and by the 49th minute they were 20 points clear – mission almost accomplished. One of the coach's power-plays reached its climax when Jared Payne knifed onto a Sexton switch pass to run under the posts. This capped an impressive debut Six Nations for the Celtic Kiwi.

Ireland were within touching distance of their goal, at which point Sexton appeared to lose his nerve – a simple penalty rebounded off the upright, another pushed wide. What was happening? 'Just a lapse of concentration,' he says. 'I was six out of six at that stage for the game and I'd felt real pressure with some of those first-half kicks as I knew every point might count. For the first miss, I allowed my mind drift ahead to the restart – should we run it back at them or play the percentages? And it rebounds off the upright. The other one was a decent strike but the wind just took it. So I was really pleased to get the chance at another shot, to bounce back, and also to put us ahead on points difference.'

Two points ahead, to be exact, with 19 minutes left on the clock. Ten minutes later, O'Brien was powering over for his second try of the game. Ian Madigan – on for Sexton at this stage – kicked the conversion and Ireland had improved their points advantage over England to 25 points. And that figure stayed the same until the final whistle, even though this looked unlikely when Stuart Hogg appeared to have scored in the right corner on 75 minutes. Mercifully for Irish supporters, the TMO correctly ruled that the Scottish full-back had lost the control of the ball – Jamie Heaslip, chasing what seemed to be a lost cause, had dislodged the ball with a well-placed and well-timed slap of his right hand. Like Sarto's try earlier, this looked like it could be a big moment on a day packed with incident. Unfortunately for Madigan, so too did his penalty miss with the final kick of the game.

Madigan was barely consolable in the dressing room, even if Sexton tried to cheer him up. We're in this together, said the older player, still miffed at having missed two penalty shots of his own. The other players weren't exactly feeling euphoric, despite having just equalled Ireland's biggest win against the Scots, home or away. How could they celebrate? Everything hinged so obviously on the game at Twickenham, which wouldn't kick off until 5.00, half an hour after the final whistle in Murrayfield. Schmidt and O'Connell said as much during a fairly meaningless press conference, before heading up to join the rest of the players and coaching team at the post-match function. Held in a huge banqueting centre, with around 400 guests, it offered a buffet plus the prospect of watching England v France on various TV monitors. The players could stomach the food, but not necessarily the rugby. The more scientific among them, like Iain Henderson, watched intently and kept a running tally. Others, like Peter O'Mahony, sat with their backs to the monitor, bent over in torture, following the contest only by the cheers – or the groans – of the other spectators.

One of the louder Irish groans came just 90 seconds into the game after Jonathan Joseph had skipped up the middle of the field to set up a try for Ben Youngs. France had conceded just two tries in the championship up to this point. Surely they weren't going to roll over now? No, they weren't. In fact after 30 minutes – around the time most of the Irish players arrived at the function – France led 15–10. They would play a full part in what was to become one of the most entertaining and most bizarre Test matches in living memory. When George Ford converted Anthony Watson's try, 10 minutes before the break, England's lead stood at two but it continued to fluctuate wildly throughout – to a nine-point advantage to 12, then back to five, up to 12 again, back to nine, up to 16, to 11, to 18, to 13, to 20 with five minutes remaining on the clock, when Ford converted Jack Nowell's second try. That made it seven tries by England to five by

France, and still time for England to nick the title.

Up in Murrayfield, we were still in the Bill McLaren suite, only taking our eyes off the TV screen during breaks in play to peek outside at the weird assembly inside the stadium, which was there thanks to the generosity of the Scottish Rugby Union and the promptings of the tournament organisers. If Ireland won, the scene needed to be set for a trophy presentation, which couldn't take place in an empty stadium, so around 10,000 supporters and revellers gathered in the stand as evening fell, watching the Twickenham game on the two giant monitors at either end of the pitch. Second-half tries by French forwards Vincent Debaty – a candidate for try of the day – and Benjamin Kayser brought riotous celebrations and chants of *Allez les Bleus*.

The punters seemed to be having a good time but upstairs, the players were in torture. 'The worst 40 minutes of my life,' says Mike Ross. 'The most nervous I've ever been,' says Sexton. 'It was as if Ben Youngs was invisible to the French players. He looked like he was going to score every time he touched the ball. But then the French would counter and score and we were going nuts, jumping up and down. Until the last few minutes anyway. I couldn't watch at that stage. A few of us were outside, just listening to how people were reacting. It was horrible.'

It had been a remarkable day's rugby, with 221 points and 27 tries over the course of three crazy games, but there remained the possibility of a final, jaw-dropping twist. England still needed seven points to nab the title. With 20 seconds on the clock, Tom Youngs throws to the lineout, six metres from the French line and the maul gathers pace as the English backs pile in. It collapses a metre short – gravity, or French lawlessness? – and when Courtney Lawes breaks away, Nick Easter is penalised by Nigel Owens (who else?) for sealing off the ruck. In Murrayfield, the Irish players are jumping around like madmen. The clock is in the red. Game over – except for the fact that Yoann Huget had tapped the ball and passed it to Uini Atonio, prompting BBC commentator Eddie Butler to utter the dreadful words: 'It could still be on for England.'

'We're roaring abuse at the telly – what the fuck are you at, Huget?' recalls Ross. 'But of course, the French don't care about us, they just want to play. Except for Rory Kockott, of course, who eventually kicked the ball off the park. He's welcome here any time!'

Owens blew his final whistle and it was official – Ireland were champions for the second year in succession. Soon the players were emerging through the Murrayfield tunnel for the second time, now in their suits, some already looking tired and emotional, to a soundtrack of U2's 'Beautiful Day' and – perhaps even more appropriately – Bon Jovi's 'Living on a Prayer'. A few minutes later, with his team-mates pogo-dancing behind him, O'Connell receives the Six Nations trophy for the second year in a row. It's a replica trophy – the real one is in London – but the emotions are real.

At his second media conference of the day, Schmidt looked even more emotionally drained, and revealed that he'd be leaving for Melbourne in a day or two with son Luke, who was due for an operation. In those circumstances, it seemed faintly ridiculous to ask him to pass judgement on a day's sport. He paid tribute to his team, naturally, but was willing to single out the Heaslip tackle on Hogg as a critical moment.

'As much as anything it's grit and character and determination,' Schmidt said. 'Jamie can make those tackles without a doubt but he could have just given up a little bit there, particularly in the context of the game. We had a good lead but we knew that every point would be precious and his determination managed to give us a level of comfort.'

But not real comfort, it should be said. 'It was tumultuous,' he said. 'Exhausting. I'm delighted on behalf of the team. I spare a thought for England. They were superb today and probably deserved a share of the spoils. I'm looking forward to being quite relaxed now but days like today build coronaries for coaches, but it also builds character. We're delighted and relieved.'

And Luke Fitzgerald? His was a story with a happy ending on a couple of levels, so naturally the media wanted to hear from him. 'I think what's good is that we went out there and we put it on the line,' he said. 'I mean, oftentimes you tighten up in those scenarios and I think it's a real lesson for any team with a favourites' tag is that you put it on the line. Try it. If you fail trying, there's absolutely no shame in that. At least you gave it a shot. That was in my mind going out onto the pitch, it might not have been in everyone else's, but that was really what I felt today. I was going to give it a shot. Because I've given up too much, it's been too long a journey back to not really have a go. And I think it really paid off.'

SCOTLAND 10, IRELAND 40
MURRAYFIELD, 21 MARCH 2015

Scotland: S Hogg; D Fife (T Visser 12–22), M Bennett (T Visser 71), M Scott (G Tonks 70), T Seymour; F Russell, G Laidlaw (capt, S Hidalgo-Clyne 56); R Grant (A Dickinson 32), R Ford (F Brown 53), E Murray (G Cross 12); J Hamilton (T Swinson 53), J Gray; A Ashe (R Harley 56), B Cowan, D Denton.
Sinbinned: Cross (56–66 mins).

Ireland: R Kearney; T Bowe, J Payne, R Henshaw, L Fitzgerald; J Sexton (I Madigan 71), C Murray (E Reddan 80); C Healy (J McGrath 53), R Best (S Cronin 62), M Ross (M Moore 53); D Toner (I Henderson 62), P O'Connell (capt); P O'Mahony, S O'Brien (J Murphy 78), J Heaslip.

Referee: J Garces (France).

Scoring sequence: 5 mins: O'Connell try, Sexton con 0–7; 10 mins: Sexton pen 0–10; 18 mins: Russell pen 3–10; 25 mins: O'Brien try, Sexton con 3–17; 29 mins: Russell try, Laidlaw con 10–17; 34 mins: Sexton pen 10–20; 45 mins: Sexton pen 10–23; 50 mins: Payne try, Sexton con 10–30; 62 mins: Sexton pen 10–33; 72 mins: O'Brien try, Madigan con 10–40.

15

ENDING AND BEGINNING

Kate Rowan

Although she dislocated her shoulder in the final match of the campaign, Hannah Tyrrell cannot help but laugh as she talks about the days and weeks following her first Six Nations title with Ireland: 'People were saying, "Did you go mad for weeks?" and I was like, "Eh, no!"' Having to do an exam less than 48 hours after returning triumphant from Scotland would put an end to any madness: 'We won the Six Nations on a Sunday; I had my arm in a sling. I actually had an exam on the Tuesday that I totally forgot about. I was totally unorganised and I had even forgotten to bring a pencil. When I was handing up my paper, the woman was like, 'Are you the Hannah Tyrrell that won the Six Nations?' and I was like 'Yeah,' and she said, 'We just had to Google to make sure it was you!' There was also little in the way of celebrations for openside flanker Claire Molloy, who flew to Dublin with the team on the Sunday night and was back at the airport at 4 a.m. on Monday to go to her job as a doctor in Cardiff. These situations were echoed across the squad. Play your sport; win or lose. Go back to work. That is the reality for an amateur athlete.

When Nora Stapleton spoke of attending an Old Belvedere function, she said that the 'old school ties and alickadoos' aspect of men's rugby in Ireland seemed alien to her experiences in the women's game. However, this older generation of men were the players of 20, 30, 40 or 50 years ago. They, like the women of today, were amateurs. Rugby fans of those generations often grumble that professionalism, while growing the game in Ireland, took away a certain purity or nobility – a sort of magic – from their sport. In a way, our Six Nations winning women are a bridge back to those times. One often hears nostalgia for the times when Tony O'Reilly would roll up to Ireland training in a Rolls-Royce, or whatever was the automobile of choice for tycoons of the day, and would be joined by team-mates from a broad spectrum of trades and professions.

As the professional game has evolved, defence has played an increasingly central role, and some of the joyful running rugby of the amateur era has been lost. Sparkling, jinking attacks that are enjoyable to watch are something that the women's game has in abundance. Stapleton is frank in comparing the visual spectacle of watching men's rugby to that of the women: 'We will never be playing the same type of rugby as the men. It is never going to look the same, simply because we are not as physical, not as quick – that is just a given – but we do play really nice rugby and that is only going to get better and better. It is about us having our brand of rugby, and people being aware that they are watching women's rugby that can't be compared to the male version that they are used to watching.' This shows that although certain aspects of the women's game provide a link with the men of the amateur era, Ireland's women are forging their own path into the future. They represent the very best of modern Ireland.

While interviewing the players, I found them to be some of the most determined, driven, tenacious and resilient people I have ever encountered. Yet they all possessed a very deep and genuine sense of humility. As a sports writer, I am acutely aware that I will never know exactly what it feels like on the field of play or in the changing rooms; I am merely taking the view of an outsider peering into this team. So, as I interviewed players I asked them if there was anything in particular they felt I should include. Often players wanted to share the chapter where I told their story with another player. Captain Niamh Briggs was adamant that second row Marie Louise Reilly – better known as Maz or Mazzie – should be mentioned: 'I am delighted to be included in this book … but for me the squad is the most important thing. They have been amazing. I don't mind if Maz gets half of my chapter because she is the best person to welcome people into the squad. She is a phenomenal rugby player, but she does so much off the pitch. I say to her all the time that it is not unseen by us. She is so funny; she is really good at making an intense situation light-hearted.

She leads on and off the pitch.' Then Paula Fitzpatrick suggested that she would prefer if the chapter coming from her point of view could be shared equally with fellow back rows Molloy and Heather O'Brien. Ailis Egan asked for something similar regarding her front row colleagues. This shows the depth of the mutual respect among members of this rugby squad. One of my few regrets in writing my part of this book is that I could not fully honour Briggs', Fitzpatrick's and Egan's requests.

To me these young women are an excellent representation of the legacy of the 'two Marys' era. For most of these players' childhoods and early adulthoods, two women were President of Ireland: Mary Robinson and then Mary McAleese. I am of a similar vintage. I remember being in primary school when McAleese was elected: at the time I didn't fully understand what my brilliant teacher, Maureen O'Donnell in St Vincent de Paul Primary School on Griffith Avenue, meant when she told our class of girls that we were lucky to be living in a time when we knew only female presidents in our young lives. Ms O'Donnell explained that it meant we could do anything, and that as we grew up we were to make sure that no one could tell us otherwise. At the time, in my naivety, I remember thinking, 'Why couldn't I do whatever I want?' I held firm to this belief all through school and college, and it was not until I started to become seriously involved in sports journalism that this belief began to waver. Before writing this book, I was seriously doubting where I fitted in as a sports writer in Ireland. I will be forever grateful to these wonderful women who inspired me back to my old belief that I should be able to do whatever I want. It may seem simplistic, but an important part of the success of this team is that as well as gifted, skilled and dedicated rugby players, it is a team of good people.

Ireland's women should not be regarded as role models just for women and girls. The game-changer in terms of growing the game and shifting perceptions is that young boys start to see them as simply rugby players, in the same way that their coach Tom Tierney does. This is already happening. Stapleton says: 'I thought it would be just the young girls who would be interested in us, but then over Easter I brought the Six Nations trophy out to a rugby camp in Munster. It was all boys. There may have been one or two girls in each group and the boys were just as interested. I was asking questions – "Anybody see the matches?" – and all the hands went up. I was like, "Can you remember any of the scores?" and they were like, "You beat Scotland 73 points to 3." The boys knew our results and had seen us play on the television. That shocked me. For me it was just about rugby now. These were 10-year-old boys: they know what we did because they are interested in rugby.'

This is the final chapter of Ireland's women's Six Nations story for 2015: the first season when women's fifteens was part of the IRFU's High Performance Unit. However, for the players, Tierney and Anthony Eddy – the IRFU's Director of Women's and Sevens Rugby – this campaign is the prologue to the story of Irish women's rugby that they want to help unfold over the next few years. The 2017 Women's Rugby World Cup, which Ireland will host, could potentially provide the climax of this story. Tierney and Eddy were emphatic that a line has been drawn under 2015's

Six Nations success. While we, the public, may wish to continue to bask in the reflected glow of the team's achievements, the reality for elite athletes is that you move on and start to plan for the next challenge.

Briggs sums up her side's ambitions: 'We want to stamp our mark on world rugby. I hope this will be a sign of things to come. I hope I am not being too unrealistic … we are not going to win every game that we play, but I want to win every game that we play and the squad wants to win every game that we play. For us to be able to do that we need to be able to go to a new level on and off the pitch: that is why this High Performance Unit for us is really important.' Stapleton sees hosting the World Cup as a logical progression built on recent seasons' successes: 'We won the grand slam, then we did well in the World Cup and then we won another Six Nations and then it's like, "What will we do next?" Well, let's bring the World Cup here and go for it and take a crack at it really. It is all about improving and promoting the sport. Not just for non-players but for players who have taken up the sport too.' Briggs continues in this vein: 'It is going to be amazing, 2017 in our own country and it is unbelievable to think where the game is coming from, to think we will be hosting the World Cup is out of this world. We have got to keep building; we have a lot of work to do before then. We have two Six Nations Championships to contend; we have got to keep building our squad to make it as strong as possible.' Egan certainly isn't mincing her words: 'My aim is to win a World Cup, and I'm planning to do that in 2017.'

If Ireland's class of 2015 proved that they are excellent rugby players, playing in a special team fired by dedication, determination and friend-ship that helped take them to Six Nations glory, I have a feeling that the coming chapters of their story will be even more riveting. I leave the final word to Stapleton: 'We thought we were committed – now there is going to be even more commitment!'

16

REFLECTIONS

Peter O'Reilly

It was a particularly giddy Ireland team bus that pulled away from the Balmoral Hotel on Sunday lunchtime, around the time that the women's team was kicking off in Cumbernauld. At the first traffic lights, it stopped alongside a coach-load of Glasgow Rangers fans from Northern Ireland, who were in Edinburgh to watch their boys take on Hibernian. Spotting the shiny green bus alongside them, fully branded to leave no one in any doubt as to the identity of the passengers, the Rangers die-hards duly banged on the windows and made as many rude gestures as they could before the light finally turned green. Another bizarre moment at the end of a bizarre but wonderful weekend.

The players found more welcoming faces at Dublin Airport – around 3,000 fans turned up to celebrate their return. But in general, there wasn't the same fuss as there had been the previous year, when the Six Nations champions were honoured at receptions in Stormont and Farmleigh House. This probably had something to do with the fact that Joe Schmidt flew out again so soon and was absent from the media in the days that followed. It might have been just an Irish thing, though. Win a trophy for the first time in a while, and you create a stir. Twice in a row? Sure, weren't you favourites to win it? No big deal.

Maybe, of course, this team was celebrated less because they were a tiny bit less lovable – no Brian O'Driscoll, not as much flair. Whereas the 2014 team had scored 16 tries in their five games, this lot managed only eight, and half of those were on Super Saturday, when normal rules most definitely didn't apply. Of those eight tries, only three were scored by backs, none of them truly memorable. Those arranging end-of-season awards dinners had a tough enough job putting the highlights reel together. In the British media coverage you sensed also a hint of begrudgery against a team winning narrowly on points difference again – and it was understandable if England supporters were a little sore, given they'd been pipped on differential for the third year running.

But look at it another way. Ireland had the best coach in the tournament, who managed his resources cleverly. It's not every set-up that can replace a world-class centre partnership with two converted full-backs and make it work. The machine kept working fairly fluently, and even when it faltered, against Wales, it recovered quickly enough to limit the damage – finishing just seven points behind the Welsh could be seen as the difference between coming first or second. Schmidt was also admirable in the way he continued to get the best out of Mike Ross – still the only player to have started every Test under the Kiwi.

Ireland had the best half-back partnership in the tournament and the best kicking game, from the hand and at restarts – they were second most successful off the kicking tee too, with 21 successes from 26 attempts. They had an inspirational captain in Paul O'Connell, who was chosen as Player of the Tournament, and leaders throughout their team – Rory Best, Peter O'Mahony, Jamie Heaslip, Rob Kearney, Murray and Sexton. They were the most disciplined team, conceding fewest penalties despite the best efforts of Wayne Barnes; critically, Les Kiss made sure they had the best defence once again – having conceded four tries in 2014, this time it was a miserly three.

Were they lucky? Undoubtedly. It would have finished differently had Welsh replacement scrum-half Gareth Davies not blown his opportunity in Rome, a couple of minutes before Leonardo Sarto's try at the other end – talk about a 14-point swing! Jamie Heaslip was rightly lionised for his try-saving tackle on Stuart Hogg five minutes from time in Edinburgh, but you could also view this as a case of pure sloppiness by a player of Hogg's ability. Finally, there was the end-game in Twickenham – that relentless English maul, grinding towards the French try-line. Could we have complained had Nigel Owens awarded a penalty try against the French for dragging it down? We've seen it happen before, and no better man than Nigel to make the call. Instead, he penalised Nick Easter for sealing off – a massive call for Ireland.

Maybe Ireland were due a break. After all, it had been Owens who dealt them a cruel blow in Christchurch nearly three years previously when they were on the cusp of a ground-breaking victory over New Zealand. It had been Owens who penalised Jack McGrath, affording the same All Blacks a chance of redemption at the Aviva Stadium. Maybe he owed us one. O'Connell admitted as much in Edinburgh – well, almost. 'I wouldn't put it down to luck, but for three games to go like that, for us to come out on top, maybe someone is smiling down on us,' O'Connell said.

So what if there was an element of good fortune? We should take what's going and cherish success when it comes. Lest it be forgotten, you have to go back 66 years to the last time Ireland won back-to-back championship titles – coincidentally, Jack Kyle and Jim McCarthy, two of the prime architects of that success, died during the course of the 2014/15 season. Older Irish rugby people remember all too well the long barren stretches, when two championship victories in the same season were a cause for celebration. Two titles in two seasons? Happy days.